A Taste
of the
Tropics

Also by Jay Solomon,
Condiments!

A Taste
of the
Tropics

**Traditional & Innovative Cooking
From the Pacific & Caribbean
by Jay Solomon**

THE CROSSING PRESS • FREEDOM, CA 95019

Copyright © 1991 by Jay Solomon
Cover and interior design by AnneMarie Arnold
Printed in the U.S.A.

6th Printing, 1999

For information on bulk purchases or group discounts for this and other Crossing Press titles, please contact our Special Sales Manager at 800/777-1048.

Visit our Web site: **www.crossingpress.com**

Library of Congress Cataloging-in-Publication Data

Solomon, Jay.
    A taste of the tropics: traditional & innovative cooking from the Pacific & Caribbean / by Jay Solomon.
        p. cm.
    Includes index.
    ISBN 0-89594-534-7 (cloth) -- ISBN 0-89594-533-9 (paper)
    1. Cookery, Caribbean 2. Cookery, Tropical 3. Caribbean Area-Social life and customs
    I. Title.
TX716.A1S55 1992
641.59729--dc20
                                                  91-43218
                                                         CIP

ACKNOWLEDGMENTS

I would like to thank my editor, Kathleen Brandes, for her encouragement and advice. I would also like to thank Elaine Goldman Gill, Dennis Hayes, and Andrea Chesman for proposing this cookbook.

The loyal customers at Jay's Cafe, the students of my Ithaca cooking classes, and my great staff have all stirred my imagination and fueled my creativity. Arlene Sarappo, manager of King's Cooking studio in New Jersey, and the students in my Verona, Bedminster, and Short Hills classes gave me an opportunity to test some of my "recipes-in-progress," and that proved to be quite illuminating and fun.

Many thanks to David Merrill of *The Herb Companion*, Paul Moomaw of *Restaurants USA*, and Dave DeWitt of *Chile Pepper* magazine for publishing my stories. And, finally, I would like to thank the following friends for supporting my culinary adventures: Janet Welch Meddleton, Robert Cima, Shaun Buckley, Jeff Lischer, Adrienne Nims, Greg Solomon, Lisa Solomon, Emily and Jessica Robin, Marion Cardwell, Margaret Shalaby, James Paradiso, Claire and Michelle Terrelonge, and Linda Meyerhoff.

Contents

This book is dedicated to my parents, Jesse and Ann Solomon.

Introduction

Welcome to a culinary excursion to the tropics. Prepare yourself for a world filled with luscious mangoes, coral papayas, tangy starfruit, island spices and herbs, pungent curries, and fiery chile peppers. A kaleidoscope of exotic tropical flavors and sensations will stimulate your taste buds and arouse your palate.

From the authentic to the innovative, the hearty to the sophisticated, tropical cuisine is an adventurous epicurean tour. You'll discover Jamaican Jerk Chicken, Indonesian Peanut Sauce, Gado-Gado, Tamarind Lamb Satay, Shrimp and Crab Pilau, Ropa Vieja, Thai Pork Curry, Callaloo, Polynesian Primavera, and Hawaiian Haupia. You'll tantalize your appetite with Tropical Fruit Vinaigrette, Sweet Plantain and Saffron-Scented Soup, Mango Salsa, Papaya Mustard Sauce, Lemongrass-Grilled Beef, Jerk Swordfish, Watermelon and Mango Mousse, and so much more.

This cookbook travels along a vast culinary bridge around the equator, starting in the Bahamas and venturing south to Cuba, Jamaica, Puerto Rico, the Virgin Islands, and then down to Barbados, Trinidad, and Aruba, and many islands in between. From the Caribbean Sea, we continue along to the Pacific Rim: to Hawaii, the South Pacific, the Philippines, and Indonesia, and then on to the shores of Thailand and Vietnam.

The nations of the tropics share a balmy climate, fertile terrain, ample rainfall, and lush, sun-drenched vegetation. The cuisines and cultures reflect a myriad of international influences: British, Dutch, French, Chinese, Indian, African, Portuguese, Japanese, and Spanish. A gastronomic melting pot.

Seafarers carried fruits and vegetables throughout the tropics: breadfruit came from the South Seas to the West Indies; bananas moved from Indo-Malaysia to the Caribbean; pineapples and chile peppers went east; and so forth. A wide variety of tropical fruits and vegetables were transplanted around the globe. Pineapples, mangoes, papayas, starfruit, citrus fruits, and chile peppers are grown throughout the tropics—along with plantains, yuca (cassava), taro, christophene (chayote), and, of course, several types of bananas.

Christopher Columbus, in search of peppercorns and other spices, hit the mother lode in the West Indies. The Caribbean islands offered a treasure of exotic spices— allspice, cloves, nutmeg, mace, cinnamon, cumin, coriander, and peppercorns. Today the islands also cultivate a variety of fresh herbs, such as thyme, lemongrass, cilantro, and chives.

The first settlers also were introduced to some of the world's fiercest chile peppers, including the notorious habañero, also known as the Scotch bonnet. Chile peppers have spread around the world; Thai peppers, known as bird peppers, have long seasoned the dishes of tropical Southeast Asia. Not surprisingly, many cooks in the tropics have a penchant for the piquant. (Not all meals are hot, however: Many Hawaiian, Filipino, Cuban, and Puerto Rican dishes are among the exceptions.)

The earthy aroma of curry, rooted in Indian cuisine, also is prevalent throughout the tropics. Thai curries evolved into spicy pastes of fresh herbs, chile peppers, and lemongrass; they often are combined with coconut milk and served with rice. Caribbean curries are mixtures of turmeric, ginger, mustard, cumin, cloves, and garlic (the mixture varies from island to island), and they often are prepared with potatoes, yams, and assorted vegetables.

Fish and shellfish are plentiful in the tropics: red snapper, grouper, blue marlin, swordfish, tuna, mahimahi, kingfish, shrimp, and conch. The meats vary from region to region—chicken is almost universal, while duck is popular along the Pacific Rim. Pork is avoided in some nations while celebrated in others. Beef is on the menus, but typically the tougher cuts are prepared and eaten in small portions.

Soy sauce, vinegar, and citrus juices are used widely. Fish sauce—an acquired taste that is similar to soy but saltier and fishier—is prevalent throughout Southeast Asia. (If you are squeamish about fishy flavors, substitute soy sauce for fish sauce.) Indonesian cuisine offers ketjap manis, a sweetened version of soy sauce.

In my quest to explore the cuisines of the tropics, I traveled widely and visited beachfront restaurants, local eateries, and roadside huts. I devoured luscious mangoes and papayas for breakfast; inhaled the warm fragrance of indigenous nutmegs, allspice berries, cinnamon, and cloves; drank coconut water right out of coconuts; and sucked the floral pulp from oozing passion fruit.

One week I grilled ahi and swordfish on a beach of Oahu, the next week I gorged on jerk chicken and pork in Jamaica. I "dined" on fried flying fish at midnight on Baxter Street on Barbados and carried a freshly caught kingfish back to a St. Martin restaurant for that night's dinner. I even consumed an entire bunch of miniature apple bananas at one sitting. And I experienced the blissful sting of chile peppers at every opportunity.

I transported the spirit of the tropics back to Jay's Cafe, my restaurant in Ithaca, where I turned up the calypso music and sauteed plantains; minced chile peppers, ginger, and lemongrass; simmered curries and chutneys; and barbecued jerk chicken. My daily specials became Jamaican Squash Bisque, Mahimahi with Papaya Salsa, Curried Blue Marlin, Aloha Chicken Salad, and Volcano Scallops with Thai Curry Sauce. I missed the pristine beaches, turquoise waters, and swaying palm trees, but I managed to create an oasis of tropical cuisines in my own kitchen.

Tropical cuisine has flair, enchantment and excitement; it is not for the meek, the timid, or the bland-at-heart. Let these recipes be your treasure maps, let your imagination be your compass. A treasure chest of fresh, healthful, and extravagant delights is buried in this cookbook. Prepare to discover the dynamic cuisines of the tropics.

Appetizers

Jerk Chicken Wings
Jamaica

Chicken wings, once relegated to fodder for mere soup stocks, now are the appetizer of choice across America. Spicy chicken wings usually bring out the fire-eating machismo that lurks beneath the surface of many people. I have risen to the occasion and prepared an ultra-spicy jerk marinade for chicken wings. (You may exercise caution and reduce or omit the chile peppers.)

Scotch bonnets, or habañeros, are becoming more and more available—Frieda's Finest is one purveyor. Caribbean grocers often carry them fresh. Frieda's carries the dried version, but I prefer to use fresh chile peppers for my recipes so I use fresh jalapeño or serrano peppers if no fresh Scotch bonnets are around.

1 cup soy sauce
1/2 cup red wine vinegar
1/2 cup vegetable oil
6 to 8 green onions
1 medium-size onion
3 to 4 Scotch bonnet or 6 jalapeño peppers, seeded and minced
1/4 cup fresh thyme leaves
2 tablespoons minced fresh ginger
2 teaspoons red hot sauce
1/4 cup brown sugar
2 tablespoons Island Seasoning (page 25), or 2 teaspoons each of ground nutmeg, cloves, and allspice
1 dozen chicken wings

In a food processor fitted with a steel blade, combine all of the ingredients except the chicken wings. Process for 10 to 15 seconds at high speed. Pour the marinade into a bowl and add the wings. Refrigerate for 4 to 6 hours, stirring after 3 hours.

Preheat the oven to 375 degrees F. Remove the wings from the marinade and place them on a rack on a baking sheet. Bake until they are browned, 15 to 20 minutes.

Arrange the chicken wings on leaf lettuce and serve immediately with cold beverages.

Yield: 2 to 4 servings

Flaming Chicken Pupus
Polynesia

Pupu (or puu puu) is the Polynesian equivalent of hors d'oeuvre. A pupu platter often is an international smorgasbord of Japanese, Korean, Thai, Hawaiian, and Polynesian delicacies. For a tropical picnic along Ala Moana Bay in Hawaii, I served chicken pupus with Taro Chips, Papaya Guacamole, and Citrus-Grilled Ahi. We then polished off a box of chocolate-covered macadamia nuts. A good time was had by all. Wasabi powder is available in Asian food stores.

1/2 cup soy sauce
1/4 cup worcestershire sauce
1/4 cup vegetable oil
1 1/2 tablespoons wasabi powder
Juice of 1 orange
1 tablespoon minced fresh ginger
1/2 tablespoon honey
1/2 teaspoon freshly ground black pepper
1 1/2 pounds skinless, boneless chicken thighs or breasts, cubed

Whisk together all of the ingredients, except the chicken, in a mixing bowl.

Place the chicken thighs in the marinade and allow to marinate for 2 to 4 hours. After 2 hours, stir the marinade.

Preheat the grill until the coals are gray to white.

Remove the chicken from the marinade and drain or shake off the excess marinade. Oil the grill lightly and place the chicken pieces on the grill. Cook for 5 to 7 minutes, then turn. Continue grilling until the chicken is cooked in the center. Remove the chicken to a serving plate and insert toothpicks in each of the cubes. Serve immediately.

Yield: 4 to 6 servings

Empanadas

Philippines

Empanadas are cousins of Caribbean patties (see Jamaican Beef Patties). These meat- or vegetable-filled turnovers are found on many Hispanic islands throughout the tropics. The Spanish gave the Philippines their name (after King Philip II) and a legacy of Mediterranean-style cooking, including this version of the beef-filled pastry.

1 pound ground pork or beef
1 medium-size onion, diced
1 to 2 cloves garlic, minced
1 cup diced, scrubbed potato
1/2 cup raisins
1/2 teaspoon freshly ground black pepper
1/4 teaspoon salt
1 pound puff pastry dough or Jamaican Beef
Patties dough (page 80)

Saute the pork (or beef) in a large skillet for 7 to 10 minutes, until the meat is brown. Remove the pork from the skillet, leaving 2 to 3 tablespoons of fat in the pan. Add the onion and garlic and saute for 2 to 3 minutes. Return the pork to the skillet, add the potato, and cook for about 15 minutes, until the potato is soft. Stir in the raisins, pepper, and salt. Remove the skillet from the heat and allow to cool.

Meanwhile, preheat the oven to 425 degrees.

Dust a work surface with flour and separate the pastry dough into 4 round balls. (For smaller empanadas, form 6 to 8 balls.) Roll the dough into circular, pizza-like sheets.

Spoon the pork mixture into the center and fold the dough over the mixture, forming a semicircular pocket. Using a fork, seal the edges of the empanada. Transfer the empanadas to a baking sheet and bake for 12 to 15 minutes, until they are golden brown. Serve with Tomatillo Hot Sauce, Sofrito, Creole Sauce, or Papaya Mustard Sauce.

Yield: 4 servings

Escovitch

West Indies

Vinegar's sharp flavor and preservative properties make it a favorite addition to fish marinades and sauces throughout the tropics. Escovitch, also called escabeche, is a method of frying fish and then marinating it in a spicy-tart pickling mixture. The fish is served hot or cold. In the South Seas version, seviche (or ceviche), the fish is marinated and served raw. In Hawaii, there is a similar dish called poke, in which seafood, often ahi (yellowfin tuna), is cubed and marinated in vinegar, soy sauce, onion, tomatoes, and green onions. In Puerto Rico, green bananas are fried and pickled.

1 1/2 pounds red snapper, mackerel, or grouper
fillets
1 lime, quartered
1 cup white vinegar
1 bell pepper, seeded and sliced
1 large onion, sliced
1 chile pepper, seeded and minced
12 allspice berries, crushed
1/4 cup oil

Place the fish in a shallow dish. Squeeze the lime over the fish and set aside for 15 minutes.

Combine the vinegar, bell pepper, onion, chile pepper, and allspice in a sauce pan. Cook over medium heat for 12 to 15 minutes, stirring occasionally.

To fry the fish, heat the oil in a large skillet. Add the fish and cook for 5 minutes, then turn. Continue cooking until the fish is done in the center.

Transfer the fish to warm plates and spoon the heated marinade over it.

Serve immediately or refrigerate for a chilled appetizer.

Yield: 4 servings

Conch Fritters

Bahamas

The Bahamas, just off the coast of Florida, could be very well be dubbed the Conch Islands. Conch fritters are served at almost every restaurant, from take-out stands to fine dining establishments. (See also Conch Chowder.) Conch is a tough meat, and mincing it for fritters has proved to be a culinary jackpot for the conch fishermen.

Conch is available fresh in Florida and the Carribbean, but canned or frozen in most of the country. Seafood purveyors often have it frozen (and it often can be special ordered). Clams can be substituted.

1 pound conch meat, coarsely chopped and blanched
1 bell pepper, seeded and minced
1 onion, minced
3 cloves garlic, minced
1 tablespoon minced fresh parsley
Zest of 1 lemon or lime
2 teaspoons red hot sauce
1 teaspoon dried thyme
1 teaspoon baking powder
1/2 teaspoon freshly ground black pepper
1/2 teaspoon salt
1 cup plus 2 tablespoons all purpose flour
2 eggs, beaten
1/4 cup milk
Vegetable oil for frying

Place the conch in a food processor fitted with a steel blade and process for 15 to 20 seconds, or until the meat is ground fine. In a large bowl, combine the conch with the remaining ingredients, forming a ball of dough. Refrigerate for at least 1 hour.

Heat oil for frying to 375 degrees. Drop spoonfuls of the conch mixture into the oil and fry until golden brown. Remove the fritters and drain on paper towels. Serve immediately with Tamarind Pepper Sauce, Tomatillo Hot Sauce, or Papaya Mustard Sauce.

Yield: 20 to 24 fritters

Mussels with Wasabi Aioli

Pacific Rim

Wasabi, also known as green horseradish, is a powder that is mixed with water to form a potent, nose-tingling paste. Although it most often is associated with Japanese sushi and sashimi, it also appears as a condiment in Southeast Asian cuisines. Its sharp, penetrating flavor is best appreciated when combined with other ingredients —in this case, garlic, ginger and lime. This condiment also makes a tangy accompaniment to other shellfish.

Wasabi Aioli
2 1/2 tablespoons wasabi powder
2 1/2 tablespoons water
1 egg yolk
1 teaspoon Dijon-style mustard
2 tablespoons lime juice
1/8 teaspoon salt
3/4 cup olive oil
6 cloves garlic, minced
2 teaspoons minced fresh ginger
1 tablespoon minced fresh parsley

2 dozen mussels

To make the aioli, first combine the wasabi powder and water to form a paste. Let stand for 5 minutes.

Blend the egg yolk for 15 seconds in a food processor fitted with a steel blade. Scrape the sides and add the mustard, lime juice, and salt. Process for another 10 seconds. Slowly drizzle in the oil while the motor is running. When half of the oil has been used, stop the processor and scrape the sides; then continue processing and drizzling.

Add the wasabi paste, garlic, ginger, and parsley and process for another 15 seconds or until all of the ingredients are fully incorporated. Scrape the aioli into a bowl, wrap tightly, and chill until you are ready to cook the mussels.

Scrub the mussels and remove the beards. In a large pot, bring to a boil about 1 inch of water. Add the mussels and cover the pot. Cook for 3 to 4 minutes, until the mussels open. Transfer the mussels to serving plates, discarding any mussels that do not open. Serve with the wasabi aioli.

Yield: 4 servings

Scallops with Wasabi Vinaigrette

Pacific Rim

This is a Pacific Rim version of seviche. The wasabi vinaigrette gently embraces the scallops, coaxing out the flavor with just a hint of heat.

3 tablespoons wasabi powder (available where Asian foods are sold)
3 tablespoons water
2 tablespoons lime juice
2 tablespoons white wine vinegar
1 teaspoon Dijon-style mustard
1/2 cup olive or vegetable oil
1 tablespoon minced fresh parsley
2 tablespoons butter
1 pound sea scallops
1 tablespoon minced fresh ginger
8 to 12 asparagus tips

Combine the wasabi powder and water to form a paste. Let stand for 5 minutes.

To make the vinaigrette, whisk together the wasabi paste, lime juice, wine vinegar, mustard, oil, and parsley.

Melt the butter in a large skillet. Add the scallops and saute over medium heat for about 7 minutes. Add the ginger and asparagus tips and saute for another 2 minutes, until the scallops are opaque in the center.

Remove the scallops and asparagus with a slotted spoon and toss with the vinaigrette. Refrigerate for 4 hours. When you are ready to serve this appetizer, remove the scallops and asparagus from the vinaigrette and arrange them over leafy greens.

Yield: 4 servings

Rum-and-Coconut Battered Shrimp

West Indies

Rum is a by-product of sugar cane, which is grown throughout the Caribbean and manufactured into sugar and molasses. The sugar is exported, and most of the molasses is used to produce rum. Although rum is enjoyed primarily as a libation, it has many culinary uses. Here it adds a warm flavor to coconut-laced batter for shrimp. Serve the shrimp with Thyme-Mustard Sauce, Papya Mustard Sauce, Tamarind Pepper Sauce, or your favorite cocktail sauce.

2 eggs
1 1/2 cups all purpose flour
1/2 cup dark rum
1/4 cup coconut milk, fresh or canned,
  unsweetened, or regular milk
1 tablespoon baking powder
1/4 teaspoon ground cloves
1/4 teaspoon ground allspice
1/4 teaspoon ground nutmeg
1/4 teaspoon freshly ground black pepper
2 cups shredded unsweetened coconut
16 medium-size shrimp, peeled and deveined
Vegetable oil for frying

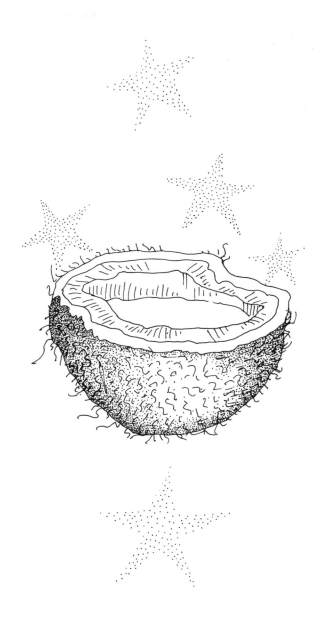

In a mixing bowl, combine the eggs, 1 cup of the flour, the rum, coconut milk, baking powder, cloves, allspice, nutmeg, and pepper. Place the remaining flour in a separate small bowl. Spread the coconut on a plate. Dredge the shrimp in the flour, then dunk it in the batter, then dredge it in the coconut. Place the coated shrimp in a single layer on waxed paper.

In a deep fryer, heat the oil to 350 degrees. Carefully drop the battered shrimp into the oil and fry for 3 to 5 minutes, until the shrimp is firm and white in the center. Drain the shrimp on paper towels and serve immediately.

Yield: 4 appetizer servings or 2 main dish servings

Pawpaw Stuffed with Shrimp

Pawpaw is another name for papaya. When papayas are green and unripe, they are used as vegetables and can be prepared in soups, sauces, and salads, or stuffed and baked. This recipe makes an exotic appetizer or first course.

2 green papayas, cut in half lengthwise, and seeded
2 tablespoons butter, melted
20 small shrimp, peeled and deveined
1 small onion, diced
1 tomato, diced
1 bell pepper, diced
1 teaspoon fresh thyme leaves
1/4 teaspoon cayenne pepper
1/4 teaspoon salt
1/2 cup shredded Gouda cheese

Preheat the oven to 350 degrees.

Scrape out the pulp from the papaya, leaving the shells intact. Dice the pulp and set aside.

Place the butter and shrimp in a skillet and cook over medium heat for about 5 minutes, or until the shrimp are white and firm. Remove the shrimp from the pan and add the papaya pulp, onion, tomato, bell pepper, thyme, cayenne, and salt. Saute over medium heat for 5 to 7 minutes. Stir in the shrimp and cook for another minute.

Fill the papaya shells with the shrimp mixture and top with the shredded cheese. Place the stuffed papayas on a baking sheet and bake for 7 to 10 minutes. Serve immediately.

Yield: 4 appetizer servings or 2 main dish servings

Papaya Guacamole

Yucatan

This is a citrusy twist on traditional guacamole. An added benefit is that this guacamole does not turn brown as fast as traditional guacamole, since the high citrus content of the papaya slows the browning process.

2 avocados, peeled and diced
1 papaya, peeled, halved, seeded, and diced
1 large tomato, diced
1 red onion, diced
2 green onions, diced
2 to 3 cloves garlic, minced
2 to 3 jalapeño peppers, seeded and minced
1 tablespoon minced fresh cilantro
1/4 cup lime juice
1 tablespoon ground cumin
1 teaspoon red hot sauce
1/4 teaspoon salt
1/4 teaspoon freshly ground black pepper
1/4 teaspoon white pepper

Place all of the ingredients in a food processor fitted with a steel blade and process for 5 to 10 seconds. Scrape the sides and process for another 10 seconds, or until the guacamole forms a chunky paste. Serve at once with Taro Chips or your favorite tortilla chips. If refrigerated, the guacamole should keep for 3 to 4 days.

Yield: 3 cups

Rasta Pasta

Jamaica

When I serve this dish as a special at my restaurant, it inevitably triggers a smile or chuckle. It's prepared with the true island spirit in mind, with lots of colorful and healthy vegetables and poignant spices. The pumpkin and coconut sauce also goes well with rice dishes. Calabaza can be found fresh at West Indian markets. Pumpkin, butternut, or acorn squash can be substituted.

4 ounces uncooked linguine or angel-hair pasta
1/4 cup butter
1 small onion, diced
2 cloves garlic, minced
2 tablespoons minced fresh ginger
1 chile pepper, seeded and minced
2 cups diced calabaza, pumpkin, butternut, or
    acorn squash
1 cup water or chicken stock
1 cup coconut milk
1 teaspoon ground coriander
1 teaspoon ground cumin
1 tablespoon thyme leaves or 1/2 teaspoon dried
    thyme
1/2 teaspoon white pepper
1/2 teaspoon ground nutmeg
1/2 teaspoon ground allspice
1/2 teaspoon salt
1 bell pepper, chopped
4 mushrooms, chopped
1/2 small zucchini, chopped
1/4 cup corn kernels, fresh, canned, or frozen and
    thawed
4 to 6 broccoli florets, blanched

Place the pasta in boiling water to cover and cook according to package directions, or until just tender, stirring occasionally. Drain the pasta and chill under cold running water. Set aside.

To make the sauce, melt 2 tablespoons of the butter over medium heat and add the onion, garlic, ginger, and chile pepper. Saute for 4 to 5 minutes. Add the pumpkin and water to the pan and cook for 15 to 20 minutes, or until the pumpkin is tender. Add the coconut milk, coriander, cumin, thyme, white pepper, nutmeg, allspice, and salt and simmer for another 4 to 5 minutes. Place the mixture in a food processor fitted with a steel blade and process for 15 seconds, until the sauce is smooth.

In a large skillet, melt the remaining butter, and add the bell pepper, mushrooms, and zucchini. Saute for 4 to 5 minutes. Add the corn and broccoli and saute for another 2 minutes. Pour the pumpkin sauce into the skillet and stir. Bring the mixture to a simmer. Cook for about 1 minute more, then blend the pasta thoroughly into the mixture. Cook for 1 to 2 minutes more, or until the pasta is steaming.

Remove the pasta to warm plates and serve with warm bread.

Yield: 4 appetizer servings or 2 main dish servings

Piquant Primavera

Polynesia

Here is a South Seas twist on the pasta primavera of nouvelle American cuisine. It's an exotic medley of crunchy vegetables, herbs, and spices. The kale will surprise you in this dish. Normally pale green and not considered a photogenic vegetable, kale turns verdant in the sauce and also gives the dish a burst of flavor and texture. For a milder version, omit the curry paste and chile peppers.

Chayote (or christophene) can be found fresh at supermarkets or Asian and Caribbean groceries and is also a Frieda's Finest product. Lemongrass is a fresh herb, found in some supermarkets and Asian food stores.

8 ounces uncooked rice noodles
2 tablespoons peanut or other vegetable oil
1 cup diced eggplant
1 cup diced zucchini or christophene
1/2 cup diced bell pepper
2 cloves garlic, minced
1 teaspoon minced fresh ginger
1 chile pepper, seeded and minced (optional)
1 teaspoon minced lemongrass
1 teaspoon red curry paste (optional)
1 cup shredded kale or bok choy
1 cup fresh bean sprouts
6 to 8 broccoli florets, blanched
2 tablespoons soy sauce or fish sauce
1 cup coconut milk, fresh or canned, unsweetened

Place the noodles in hot water to cover for 5 minutes. Drain in a colander and cool under running water.

Heat the oil in a large skillet. Add the eggplant, zucchini, and bell pepper and saute for 4 to 5 minutes, until the vegetables are soft. Add the garlic, ginger, chile pepper, lemongrass, and curry paste and saute for another 2 minutes. Add the kale, bean sprouts, broccoli, soy sauce, and coconut milk and cook for 3 to 5 minutes, stirring frequently. Add the rice noodles and cook until the noodles are steaming, continuing to stir. Serve with Coconut-Macadamia Bread, Maui Onion Bread, or Christophene-Carrot Bread.

Yield: 4 servings

MILKING A COCONUT

To make coconut milk, first prepare yourself mentally and physically for a small challenge. Then, puncture one of the coconut's "eyes" with an ice pick or large nail. Drain the liquid into a bowl. This is coconut water, not milk. Place the coconut in the oven and roast for 15 to 20 minutes at 375 degrees F.

Cool the coconut, then use a hammer or mallet to whack it into several pieces. (Play it safe and cover the coconut with a cloth before you strike it.) Pry the white flesh from the broken shell and peel off the brown skin.

Next, puree or shred the coconut pieces in a food processor fitted with a steel blade. Add 2 to 4 cups of hot water to the pureed coconut and allow to steep for 30 minutes. (You may include the coconut water as part of the mixture.) To produce richer milk, use less water.

Strain the steeped coconut mixture through a cheesecloth, pressing firmly to release as much liquid as possible. Discard the solids and use or refrigerate the coconut milk.

There is an easier method: Purchase canned coconut milk. It is available in most Asian and Caribbean grocery stores and is becoming more widely available nationwide. To prepare the recipes in this book, purchase *unsweetened* coconut milk, not cream of coconut (which is intended for pina coladas).

Island Coconut Chips

West Indies

Roasted coconut chips are popular snacks in the Caribbean. Although they typically are salted (a version of potato chips), I find that the seasonings of clove, nutmeg, allspice, and cinnamon add a delightful island touch. Serve the coconut chips as an afternoon munchie with tropical drinks or other appetizers.

1 coconut, shell removed
1 teaspoon Island Seasoning

Preheat the oven to 375 degrees.

Pierce the coconut's eyes and drain the milk. Save the milk for other uses, or drink it. Whack open the coconut and peel the brown surface off the meat. With a vegetable peeler or grater, remove long, wide strips of coconut. Spread out the chips onto a lightly greased baking sheet. Sprinkle the Island Seasoning evenly over the chips and bake for about 10 minutes, until the chips begin to brown.

Yield: 2 to 4 servings

ISLAND SEASONING

My first trip to the Caribbean was to Sint Maarten, an island half Dutch and half French. (The French side is referred to as St. Martin.) Aside from being swept away by the sandy beaches and exotic terrain, I was introduced to an abundance of spices—allspice berries, whole cloves, nutmeg and its outer covering, mace, cinnamon bark, and peppercorns. All were sold at the local street markets, along with local fruit and vegetables. Until then, as far as I knew, those spices could have grown in a can. It was something of a revelation to discover that they were harvested in the Caribbean. My appreciation for the seasonings took a quantum leap forward. The spices became such a large part of my culinary repertoire that I created this special Island Seasoning mixture. Sprinkle it over soups, chutneys, fried plaintains, curry dishes, grilled chicken or fish, and steamed vegetables.

1 tablespoon ground allspice
1 tablespoon ground nutmeg
1 tablespoon ground cloves
1/2 tablespoon ground cinnamon
1/2 tablespoon ground mace
1 teaspoon dried thyme
1 teaspoon freshly ground black pepper

Combine all of the ingredients in a small mixing bowl. Spoon the seasonings into a container with a sieve-top. Store in a cool, dry place.

Yield: About 1 cup

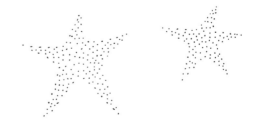

Taro Chips

West Indies

Taro (also known as tannia, cocoyam, coco, and dasheen) is a tuber with fibrous skin and milky white flesh with occasional brownish-purple streaks. In the Caribbean, the leaves of the taro plant are used for callaloo; in the Pacific, the leaves are called luau and cooked like spinach. The tuber can be roasted, boiled, fried into chips, or cooked and mashed into Hawaiian poi.

Taro chips make a quick and easy tropical snack. For a real treat, thinly slice and fry a green plantain with the taro. Dip the chips in Papaya Guacamole or Lime-Peanut Dipping Sauce.

Taro root is available in the specialty produce section of supermarkets—Frieda's Finest is a nationwide distributor. Also at Asian and West Indian grocers.

1 pound taro
4 cups vegetable oil for frying
1/8 teaspoon ground cayenne pepper or Scotch
  bonnet pepper (optional)

Heat the oil in a heavy stockpot until it is at 375 degrees.

Peel the taro and slice it into paper-thin wafers. Drop half of the taro slices into the oil and fry for 10 minutes, until the chips are light brown. Remove the chips with a slotted spoon and arrange in a single layer on a plate lined with a paper towel. Fry the remaining taro slices. Sprinkle the pepper over the fried chips.

Yield: 4 servings

POI PONDERING

Poi is the mashed potatoes of Hawaii. Well, sort of. Made from the root of the taro plant, poi is quite bland, with the consistency of baby food. Sounds yummy, right? Actually, poi should be eaten with highly seasoned foods, as it absorbs the other flavors well and provides enough sustenance for a meal. Some people have compared poi to brown wallpaper paste, but that's not quite true. Just make sure not to eat it by itself.

Taro can also be made into chips or flour. The leaves of the plant are cooked like spinach. Taro grows in paddies or wetlands that must be kept constantly moist during the long growing season. Taro is not readily available on the mainland, but potatoes can be used as a substitute.

Soups

Chicken and Noodle Soup

Pacific Rim

The chicken and noodle soup of the Pacific Rim is a combination of chicken, lemongrass, ginger, garlic, fish sauce, lime juice, leafy green vegetables, and cellophane or rice noodles. The broth is rich with herbal fragrances and palate-warming sensations.

4 ounces cellophane or rice noodles
1 chicken, about 3 pounds, cut into 6 to 8 pieces
8 cups water
1 large onion, diced
2 cups chopped celery
2 tablespoons vegetable oil
1 tablespoon minced fresh lemongrass
2 cloves garlic, minced
2 teaspoons minced fresh ginger
1 chile pepper, seeded and minced
4 green onions, chopped
1 cup shredded bok choy, kale, or Chinese cabbage
1/4 cup fish sauce
2 tablespoons lime juice
1 tablespoon minced fresh cilantro

Place the cellophane noodles in hot water for 3 minutes, then drain. Cut the noodles into 2-inch sections.

Combine the chicken pieces, water, onion, and celery in a large stockpot. Bring to a boil and cook for 30 to 35 minutes over moderately high heat. Transfer the chicken to a plate and strain the stock through a sieve into a mixing bowl. Keep the stock and discard the vegetables.

After the chicken cools, remove the meat from the bones. Dice the meat and add it to the stock.

Clean the stock pot. In it, place the oil, lemongrass, garlic, ginger, and chile pepper and saute over medium heat for 2 to 3 minutes, until the vegetables are soft. Return chicken and stock to the stockpot and add the green onions, bok choy, fish sauce, and lime juice. Bring the soup to a simmer. Add the cooked noodles and cilantro and cook for another 4 to 5 minutes over medium heat, stirring occasionally.

To serve, transfer the noodles (with tongs or a large slotted spoon) to soup bowls and ladle the soup over the noodles.

Yield: 6 to 8 servings

Jakarta Chicken Soup

Indonesia

As in the Caribbean islands, chickens run free throughout Indonesia and the rest of Southeast Asia. The meat is tough but very tasty, and ideal for Indonesian soups. This version always elicits compliments.

2 tablespoons peanut or vegetable oil
1 medium-size onion, diced
2 cloves garlic, minced
1 to 2 chile peppers, seeded and minced
1 tablespoon minced fresh ginger
1 tablespoon minced fresh lemongrass
4 cups chicken stock
1 pound skinless, boneless, cooked chicken meat, diced
1 1/2 cups coconut milk, fresh or canned, unsweetened
1/3 cup peanut butter
1/4 cup soy sauce or ketjap manis
1/4 cup lime juice
1/4 cup roasted unsalted peanuts, crushed
1 teaspoon ground coriander
1 teaspoon ground cumin
1/2 teaspoon freshly ground black pepper

In a large saucepan, heat the oil and add the onion, garlic, chile pepper, ginger, and lemongrass. Saute for 4 to 6 minutes over medium heat, until the onion is soft and translucent. Add the chicken stock and diced chicken and simmer for 12 to 15 minutes, stirring occasionally. Reduce the heat and add the coconut milk, peanut butter, soy sauce, lime juice, peanuts, coriander, cumin, and black pepper. Simmer for 5 to 10 minutes, stirring frequently. Ladle into soup bowls and serve immediately.

Yield: 6 to 8 servings

Callaloo

West Indies

Callaloo (also known as calalou) is served in a variety of guises throughout the Caribbean. Every island's recipe, however, includes the leaves of the taro (dasheen) plant, also called callaloo. Callaloo soup can be made with pork, chicken, crabmeat, okra, pumpkin, yams, yuca, plantains, coconut milk, and whatever else is in the kitchen. Sometimes it's pureed and sometimes its not. After sampling a variety of callaloo soups on my travels, I've settled on this version. Spinach or Swiss chard can be substituted for taro leaves. Callaloo is a leaf that is sold canned at Caribbean markets. Occasionally it is fresh.

1/4 pound salt pork
1 large onion, diced
1 chile pepper, seeded and minced
1 clove garlic, minced
1/2 pound boneless pork loin, diced
4 cups chicken stock
1/2 pound callaloo, spinach, or Swiss chard leaves
1 cup diced pumpkin or butternut squash
1 teaspoon dried thyme
1/2 teaspoon freshly ground pepper
1/2 pound lump crabmeat, cartilage removed

Add the salt pork to a saucepan and cook over medium heat for about 10 minutes, stirring occasionally. Remove the salt pork and discard, leaving the rendered fat in the pan. Add the onion, chile pepper, garlic, and pork loin to the pan and saute for 8 to 10 minutes, until the pork is cooked in the center.

Add the chicken stock, callaloo, calabaza, thyme, and black pepper to the pan. Cook for 15 minutes over moderately high heat, stirring occasionally. Reduce the heat to medium, stir in the crabmeat, and cook for another 10 minutes.

Ladle into bowls and serve immediately with Taro Chips, Pumpkin and Black-Eyed Pea Accras, Maui Onion Bread, or Chile Pepper Corn Bread.

Yield: 4 servings

Conch Chowder

Bahamas

Eating conch is a favorite Bahamian pastime. The conch boats arrive early in the morning, and the conchs are sold off the boats at the marina. Once the conch is expelled from its shell, it can be made into a fresh salad, fried as fritters, or stewed in chowder. Although fresh conch can be difficult to find, frozen or canned conch may be used for chowder. The shells are sold as souvenirs at straw markets. This is my favorite way to eat conch. (See also Conch Fritters.)

Roux

2 tablespoons butter
2 tablespoons all-purpose flour

Chowder

2 tablespoons butter, melted
1 medium-size onion, diced
1 bell pepper, seeded and minced
2 cloves garlic, minced
1 Scotch bonnet or jalapeño pepper, seeded and minced
2 tablespoons curry powder
1 teaspoon freshly ground black pepper
1 teaspoon salt
2 sweet potatoes, scrubbed and diced
4 cups water
1 pound conch meat, diced
1/4 cup canned crushed tomato
1 cup light cream

For the roux, add 2 tablespoons of the butter to a skillet and slowly stir in the flour, cooking over low heat. Cook for 3 to 4 minutes, stirring frequently. The roux should resemble an off-white paste. Set aside.

To prepare the chowder, place the melted butter, onion, bell pepper, garlic, and Scotch bonnet in a saucepan and saute for about 5 minutes over medium heat. Add the curry powder, black pepper, and salt and saute for another 2 minutes. Add the sweet potatoes, water, conch, and crushed tomatoes and simmer for 20 to 25 minutes. Stir in the light cream and return to a simmer. Whisk in the roux and continue to simmer for 3 minutes, stirring frequently. Ladle into soup bowls and serve immediately with Chile Pepper Corn Bread or Maui Onion Bread.

Yield: 6 to 8 servings

SCOTCH BONNET PEPPER: CAPSICUM JEWEL OF THE CARIBBEAN

The Scotch bonnet is a small, round, and rumpled chile pepper with a powerful sting and an aromatic, floral flavor. It is the hottest pepper in the world, more than a hundred times hotter than the jalapeño. On a heat scale of 1 to 10, a red bell pepper rates at 1, jalapeño at 5, serrano at 7, and Scotch bonnet checks in at 10. Shaped like a lantern, Scotch bonnets come in bright orange, yellow, and green. The Scotch bonnet is grown throughout the Caribbean, the Yucatan, and parts of Central and South America. It is also known as habañero (Spanish for *from Havana*), Bahama mama, and Mrs. Jake's Bottom.

Scotch bonnets are grown mostly in backyards throughout the Caribbean. The chile peppers flavor a variety of dishes, from conch salad and curried scallops to jerk chicken and chile corn bread. They have also inspired an array of Caribbean hot sauces, most of which leave your tongue with a blistering—and, to some, blissful—sting.

As with other chile peppers, it is essential to use rubber or plastic gloves when handling these peppers. Removing the seeds will temper the flame slightly. If you have more peppers then you need, puree the extra ones with a little vinegar and refrigerate; the pepper mash will last longer than fresh peppers.

Groundnut Stew

West Indies

Groundnuts—also known as earth nuts, goober peas, and the more familiar peanuts—turn up in a variety of stews and sauces throughout the tropics. Technically, peanuts are legumes, like peas and beans. The plant produces tiny, pea-shaped flowers above the ground; after pollination, it buries the seed pods in the ground to ripen (hence the name).

I prefer natural peanut butter for most recipes; commercial peanut butter often contains salt, sugar, and other additives. When natural peanut butter separates during storage (the oil rises to the top), stir it vigorously before use. Refrigerating the peanut butter will reduce the degree of separation.

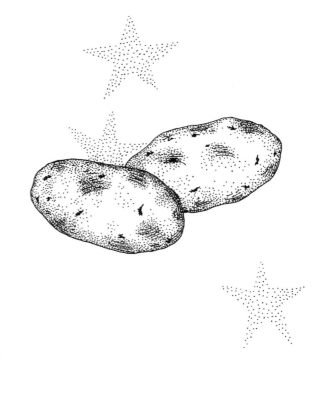

2 tablespoons butter or vegetable oil
1 medium-size onion, diced
2 cloves garlic, minced
1 tablespoon minced fresh ginger
2 small potatoes, diced
1 cup yuca or potato, peeled and diced
5 cups water
2 cups unsweetened chunky peanut butter
1/4 cup canned crushed tomato
1 cup shredded kale or spinach
1/2 cup chopped okra
2 teaspoons dried thyme
2 teaspoons ground cumin
1 teaspoon freshly ground black pepper
1/4 teaspoon salt
1 tablespoon minced fresh cilantro

Saute the butter, onion, garlic, and ginger in a stockpot. Add the potatoes, yuca, and water and cook for 15 to 20 minutes over medium heat, until the vegetables are soft. Add the peanut butter, crushed tomatoes, kale, okra, and seasonings and bring to a simmer, stirring frequently. If the peanut butter clumps together, whisk the mixture. Remove from the heat and serve in soup bowls.

Yield: 6 to 8 servings

Black Bean Soup

Cuba

Cuba is a mystery to many Americans, since trade and tourist travel are not permitted with the Communist nation. Yet it is the largest Caribbean island, located not far from the coast of Florida. In culinary circles, Cuba is known for its delectable black bean soup. Black beans have an earthy taste that blend well with cumin, garlic, chile peppers, and cilantro.

8 ounces black beans, rinsed and soaked overnight in water to cover
7 to 8 cups vegetable stock, low sodium chicken stock, or water
1/2 cup flat beer
1/4 cup dark rum
4 cloves garlic, minced
2 medium-size onions, diced
2 tablespoons butter
1 cup finely chopped celery
1 green bell pepper, seeded and diced
1 red bell pepper, seeded and diced
1 to 2 Scotch bonnet or jalapeño peppers, seeded and minced
2 large carrots, peeled and diced
1/2 cup canned crushed tomatoes
1 1/2 tablespoons ground cumin
1 teaspoon red hot sauce
1/2 tablespoon chili powder
1/2 teaspoon freshly ground black pepper
1/2 teaspoon salt
1/4 teaspoon cayenne pepper
1 tablespoon minced fresh cilantro

Drain the black beans and combine in a heavy saucepan with the stock, beer, rum, garlic, and half of the onions. Bring to a simmer. Cook for 1 to 2 hours over low flame, stirring occasionally. If the stock evaporates too quickly, reduce the heat, add up to 2 cups of hot water, and continue simmering.

Melt the butter in a saucepan and add the remaining onions, plus the celery, peppers, and carrots. Saute over medium heat until the vegetables are soft but not mushy, 5 to 7 minutes. Set aside.

When the beans are soft, puree half of the mixture in a food processor fitted with a steel blade. Return the puree to the saucepan and add the sauteed vegetables, crushed tomatoes, and seasonings. Bring to a simmer and cook for about 15 minutes, stirring occasionally. Add a little hot water or rum if it is too thick, or continue to simmer if it is too thin. Serve at once with yogurt or sour cream.

Yield: 4 to 8 servings

Jamaican Squash Bisque

West Indies

This bisque combines the enticing Caribbean flavors of rum, coconut, island spices, and West Indian squash (also known as calabaza). The squash is so large that it often is sold in wedges in Caribbean marketplaces. Its flesh is vibrant orange, with a streaked, dark-green skin, and it tastes rather like butternut squash. Other orange-fleshed squashes are acceptable substitutes in this recipe.

1 tablespoon butter
1 medium-size onion, diced
1 cup diced celery
2 cloves garlic, minced
1 chile pepper, seeded and minced (optional)
1 tablespoon minced fresh ginger
4 cups peeled and diced calabaza, American
   pumpkin, or butternut or acorn squash
4 cups water
2 cups coconut milk, fresh or canned, unsweetened
1/4 cup dark rum
1 tablespoon ground cumin
2 teaspoons ground coriander
1 teaspoon fresh thyme leaves
1/2 teaspoon ground allspice
1/2 teaspoon salt
1/2 teaspoon freshly ground black pepper
1/4 teaspoon white pepper

In a large saucepan, melt the butter. Add the onion, celery, garlic, chile pepper, and ginger. Saute over medium heat for 5 to 7 minutes, until the vegetables are soft. Add the pumpkin and water to the saucepan and simmer for 15 to 20 minutes, stirring occasionally. Reduce the heat and add the coconut milk, rum, cumin, coriander, thyme, allspice, salt, and black and white pepper. Cook for another 5 to 7 minutes, stirring occasionally, until the soup is steaming. Transfer the soup to a food processor fitted with a steel blade and process for 15 to 20 seconds. Pour the bisque immediately into soup bowls. Serve with Chile Pepper Corn Bread.

Yield: 6 to 8 servings

Papaya, Mint, and Coconut Soup

West Indies

Here is a refreshing summertime soup with the smooth tropical flavors of coconut and papaya. With each chilled spoonful, the mint lingers ever-so-gracefully on the tip of the tongue.

2 ripe papayas, peeled, seeded, and chopped
2 cups coconut milk, fresh or canned, unsweetened
2 tablespoons dark rum
2 tablespoons mint leaves
2 teaspoons honey
1 teaspoon Island Seasoning (page 25) or 1/4
   teaspoon each of ground clove, nutmeg,
   allspice, and white pepper

Place all of the ingredients in a food processor fitted with a steel blade and process for 20 to 30 seconds, until the mixture is smooth. Refrigerate for at least 1 hour before serving. Garnish with a mint sprig.

Yield: 4 servings

Yuca and Tomato Stew

Jamaica

Yuca is the tuberous root that gives the world tapioca. Also known as cassava and manioc, yuca has a waxy, brown skin and white, starchy flesh. Yuca can be fried, boiled, or mashed; it can be shredded and baked into bread or a cake known as "bammy." (The juice extracted from yuca is called cassareep, which is traditionally used as a preservative, as well as an ingredient in Caribbean pepperpot stew.) Yuca is a cheap filler, a good source of carbohydrates, and a good staple for a hearty soup or stew. You can find yuca in the specialty produce section of supermarkets and also at Caribbean grocers.

2 tablespoons vegetable oil
1 medium-size onion, diced
1 medium-size bell pepper, seeded and diced
1 cup diced celery or broccoli stalk
1 cup diced eggplant
2 cloves garlic, minced
1 chile pepper, seeded and minced
1 cup peeled, diced yuca or potato
1 cup diced pumpkin or butternut squash
8 cups vegetable stock or water
1 tablespoon fresh thyme leaves or 2 teaspoons
  dried thyme
1 teaspoon freshly ground black pepper
1/2 teaspoon salt
1 cup diced okra
1/2 cup canned crushed tomato
2 cups shredded Swiss chard leaves
1/2 cup cooked pigeon peas or kidney beans
1/2 cup fresh herbs, such as chives, tarragon,
  oregano, or marjoram

Place the oil, onion, bell pepper, celery, eggplant, garlic, and chile pepper in a saucepan and saute over medium heat for about 7 minutes, until the vegetables are soft. Add the yuca, pumpkin, stock, thyme, pepper, and salt. Simmer for 20 to 25 minutes, stirring occasionally. Add the okra after 15 minutes.

Reduce the heat and stir in the crushed tomatoes, Swiss chard, pigeon peas, and herbs. Bring the soup to a simmer and cook for another 5 minutes, stirring frequently. Serve immediately.

Yield: 6 to 8 servings

Christophene and Corn Chowder

West Indies

The mild flavor and firm texture of the christophene make it a popular ingredient for Caribbean soups and stews.

Roux

2 tablespoons butter
2 tablespoons all-purpose flour

Chowder

2 tablespoons butter, melted
2 christophenes or medium-size zucchini, unpeeled and diced
1/2 cup diced celery
1 medium-size onion, diced
1 medium-size bell pepper, seeded and diced
2 cloves garlic, minced
1 jalapeño pepper, seeded and minced
1 large potato, scrubbed and diced
4 cups water
1/4 cup dry sherry
1 tablespoon ground cumin
1 tablespoon paprika
1 tablespoons minced fresh parsley
1 teaspoon dried thyme
1 teaspoon dried oregano
1/2 teaspoon freshly ground black pepper
1/2 teaspoon white pepper
1/2 teaspoon salt
1 cup diced okra
1 cup light or heavy cream
1 cup corn kernels, fresh, canned, or frozen and thawed

To make the roux, place the butter in a skillet over low heat. When it melts, gradually stir in the flour. Continue to stir, forming a smooth paste. Cook for about 5 minutes, stirring frequently. Remove the roux from the heat and set aside.

To prepare the chowder, place the melted butter, christophenes, celery, onion, bell pepper, garlic, and chile pepper in a saucepan and saute over medium heat for 10 minutes. Add the diced potato, water, sherry, cumin, paprika, parsley, thyme, oregano, black and white pepper, and salt and simmer for 15 to 20 minutes, stirring occasionally.

Add the okra and continue simmering for another 10 minutes, or until a fork easily pierces the potatoes. Add the cream and corn and return to a simmer, stirring occasionally. Reduce heat and gradually whisk in the roux. Simmer for another 2 to 3 minutes. Ladle into soup bowls and serve immediately.

Yield: 8 servings

THYME TO EAT

In the islands of the Caribbean, bunches of thyme are sold at street markets, tucked among plantains, mangoes, and breadfruits. The tiny, oval petals exude an earthy, penetrating, and almost magical aroma. Thyme is the herbal liasion between hot and sweet, spicy and delicate flavors—balancing the sweet island spices of nutmeg, cloves, cinnamon, and allspice and slightly tempering the heat of Scotch bonnet peppers. Thyme gives jerk chicken its earthy, pungent flavor.

Unlike many fresh herbs, thyme retains its flavor during the cooking process, making it a favorite for hearty stews, marinades, stocks, breads, sauces, and soups. It also retains much of its potent aroma in the dried form. Common thyme, or English thyme, is the most prevalent variety. The leaves can be stripped off the woody stem, against the grain, in one smooth motion. Pulling off the leaves with your hands will stamp your fingers with thyme's cologne, a fragrance easily as delicious as garlic or basil.

Sweet Plantain and Saffron-Scented Soup

West Indies

Ripe plantains will exhibit an off-yellow color with scattered patches of black and brown, and sometimes a white growth at the tip. Do not be alarmed. Despite their appearance, mature plantains are quite sweet and tasty, a cross between a banana and a potato. Mature plantains make a sweet and fragrant soup, especially when accented with saffron, ginger, and rum. Plantains are available at the specialty produce section of supermarkets, often near the bananas.

2 1/2 tablespoons butter
2 tablespoons minced fresh ginger
2 to 3 shallots, minced
1 medium-size onion, diced
2 large ripe plantains, peeled and chopped
2 1/2 cups water
2 cups light cream or milk
1/4 cup dark rum
1/2 teaspoon crumbled saffron threads
1/4 teaspoon ground allspice
1/4 teaspoon ground cloves
1/4 teaspoon ground nutmeg
1/4 teaspoon salt
1/8 teaspoon cayenne pepper

In a saucepan, melt the butter. Add the ginger, shallots, and onion and saute over medium heat for 4 to 5 minutes. Add the plantains and water and simmer for 10 to 12 minutes, stirring occasionally. Reduce the heat and add the light cream, rum, and seasonings. Return the mixture to a simmer, then remove from the heat.

Pour the soup into a blender or food processor fitted with a steel blade and process for 15 to 20 seconds, until the soup is smooth. Serve immediately with Coconut-Macadamia Bread.

Yield: 6 to 8 servings

Breadfruit Vichyssoise

Jamaica

It was breadfruit that Captain Bligh was attempting to transport from the South Seas to the West Indian islands in 1787. The *Mutiny on the Bounty* set Captain Bligh adrift, but he survived and in 1793 planted the first trees on St. Vincent. Breadfruit is about the size of a soccer ball, and it can be boiled, roasted, or grilled. It also makes a simple, delicious, and substantial chilled soup.

One morning in Jamaica, en route to a straw market, I pulled over at a squatter's garden. The squatter gave me a tour of his tropical vegetation: He had everything, from eggplants and Scotch bonnets to callaloo and plantains. He also offered to share his breakfast—breadfruit that had been roasted and charred on the barbecue. All I could think of was, this isn't Kansas, Dorothy: A meal of charred breadfruit in the middle of a tropical garden was a long and exotic way from home.

Breadfruit is available canned and fresh at Caribbean grocery stores. Potatoes can be substituted.

2 tablespoons butter
1 medium-size onion
1 clove garlic, minced
2 cups chopped, peeled breadfruit
4 cups water or vegetable stock
1 cup plain yogurt
2 tablespoons minced fresh dill
2 tablespoons minced fresh chives
1/2 teaspoon white pepper
1/2 teaspoon salt

Place the butter in a saucepan and saute the onion and garlic for 4 to 5 minutes. Add the breadfruit and water and cook over medium heat for about 15 minutes, until the breadfruit is tender. Remove from the heat and chill.

Add the cooled mixture, plus the yogurt and seasonings, to a food processor fitted with a steel blade. Process for 20 to 30 seconds, or until the mixture is smooth. Serve immediately or refrigerate until ready to serve.

Yield: 4 to 6 servings

Fish &
Shellfish

Red Snapper with Tamarind-Pineapple Sauce

Pacific Rim

A successful sauce coaxes out the flavor of the main dish while maintaining its own distinct presence. This sauce does exactly that. Tamarind's mildly sour flavor—tempered by the sweetness of pineapple and the tartness of vinegar—enhances the flavor of the fish without overpowering it. The sauce also goes very well with tuna, grouper, and swordfish steaks.

Tamarind pulp is available at specialty grocery stores or Asian food stores.

Sauce

8 ounces dried tamarind pulp
1 1/2 cups water
2 tablespoons butter, melted
2 cups diced fresh pineapple
1 onion, diced
3 green onions, minced
1 tomato, diced
1 clove garlic, minced
2 tablespoons brown sugar
1/2 teaspoon freshly ground black pepper
1/2 teaspoon dried thyme
1/4 teaspoon ground cloves
1/4 teaspoon ground allspice
1/4 teaspoon salt
1 tablespoon minced fresh cilantro

4 red snapper fillets, about 8 ounces each
1/2 cup all-purpose flour
2 tablespoons vegetable oil
4 wedges fresh pineapple

To make the sauce, combine the tamarind and water in a saucepan and bring to a simmer, stirring frequently. Cook for 5 minutes, then drain, reserving the liquid and discarding the pulp.

Add the butter, pineapple, onion, green onions, tomato, and garlic to a saucepan and saute over medium heat for 8 to 10 minutes. Add the tamarind liquid, brown sugar, pepper, thyme, cloves, allspice, and salt to the pan and simmer for 15 minutes, stirring occasionally. The sauce should thicken to the consistency of chutney.

Stir in the cilantro. Keep the sauce warm until the fish is cooked or refrigerate until ready to use.

To prepare the fish, heat the oil in a large skillet. Dredge the fillets lightly in the flour and place in the skillet. Cook over medium heat for 7 to 9 minutes on each side.

Remove the fillets to warm serving plates and spoon the tamarind-pineapple sauce over the top. Serve immediately, garnished with a wedge of pineapple. Pass the extra sauce at the table.

Yield: 4 servings

Baked Opakapaka

Hawaii

Opakapaka, also known as pink snapper, is one of the many exotic, delicate fish caught off the shores of Hawaii. A light marinade of fresh herbs and coconut milk is a popular way to cook this fish. Red snapper or trout is an appropriate substitute.

1 1/2 cups coconut milk, fresh or canned, unsweetened
1/2 cup lime juice
1/2 cup dry white wine
1/4 cup soy sauce
1/4 cup mint leaves, chopped
2 tablespoons minced fresh cilantro
1/2 teaspoon saffron threads
1 1/2 pounds whole pink snapper, red snapper, or trout, cleaned

In a shallow bowl, combine the coconut milk, lime juice, wine, soy sauce, mint leaves, cilantro, and saffron. Marinate the fish for 3 to 4 hours. Turn the fish after 2 hours.

Preheat the oven to 375 degrees.

Remove the fish from the marinade and wrap in aluminum foil. Place the package on a sheet pan and bake for 15 to 20 minutes, or until the flesh flakes easily. Unwrap the fish and serve on a large platter.

Yield: 4 servings

DOING THE LUAU

A luau is a lavish Polynesian feast of song, dance—and most of all—food. Kalua pig, lomi lomi salmon, laulau, poi, and haupia (coconut pudding) are the traditional fare at a luau. In Old Hawaii, a pit was dug and lined with sizzling stones, lava rocks, tree stumps, and wet ti or banana leaves. This became an imu, or underground oven. A whole pig was then lowered into the pit and roasted slowly. The leaves prevented scorching, and water was poured through a bamboo tube to create steam.

The roasted kalua pig is served with lomi lomi salmon—a chilled dish of salted salmon, tomatoes, and onions—and poi. Laulau—a package of shredded pork and butterfish wrapped in banana leaves—and breadfruit and yams are also cooked in the pit. Luaus are celebration for any type of of festive occasion: birthdays, holidays, farewells, you name it.

Today, commercial luaus are very popular on the islands. These glitzy replicas of the traditional festival offer ukulele bands, hula dancers, and roast suckling pigs as the buffet's centerpiece.

Blaff

Bahamas

This dish is named after the sound the fish makes when it hits the skillet: BLAFF! In the Bahamas, the fishermen eat blaff for breakfast on the decks of their boats. The poaching liquid is served with the fish as a sauce. This is an extremely healthful way to prepare fish.

5 cups water
3/4 cup lime juice
1 1/2 pounds red snapper, marlin, or swordfish
1/2 cup diced onion
2 cloves garlic, minced
1 whole Scotch bonnet pepper
1 tablespoon minced fresh parsley
1 tablespoon fresh thyme leaves
1 teaspoon allspice berries
1 teaspoon salt

Combine 1 cup of the water and 1/2 cup of the lime juice in a shallow baking dish. Add the fish and marinate for 2 hours, turning after 1 hour. After marinating, drain the fish and discard the marinade.

In a saucepan, place the remaining 4 cups of water, 1/4 cup of lime juice, onion, garlic, Scotch bonnet pepper, parsley, thyme, allspice berries, and salt. Bring to a rolling boil over high heat. Boil for 3 to 4 minutes, then add the fish. Simmer for 8 to 10 minutes, until the fish is done in the center and flakes easily when pulled with a fork.

With a slotted spatula, remove the fish from the poaching liquid. Transfer to warm plates. Remove the Scotch bonnet from the broth. Spoon the broth over the fish and serve immediately.

Yield: 4 servings

Citrus-Grilled Ahi

Hawaii

Ahi is the Hawaiian name for yellowfin tuna. The flesh is deep burgundy red, with a steaklike texture that is ideal for grilling. On the beach at Ala Moana Bay in Honolulu, I lightly marinated and barbecued fresh ahi. It was a postcard spot—the sun setting, palm trees swaying, and the fish steaks on the barby. The ahi melted in our mouths.

1 cup orange juice
1 cup grapefruit juice
1/4 cup lime juice
1/2 cup dry sherry
1 tablespoon fresh thyme leaves
1/4 teaspoon cayenne pepper
1/4 teaspoon salt
1 1/2 pounds ahi, kingfish, swordfish, or mahimahi steaks
1 tablespoon paprika

Combine the citrus juices, sherry, thyme, cayenne, and salt in a shallow baking dish. Add the fish and refrigerate for 4 hours, turning the steaks after 2 hours.

Preheat the grill until the coals are gray to white.

Remove the fish from the marinade. Lightly oil the grill and place the fish over the heat. Lightly sprinkle paprika over the fish. Turn after 5 to 7 minutes. Continue grilling for 5 to 7 minutes more, or until the fish is opaque in the center.

Remove the fish to warm plates and serve immediately.

Yield: 4 servings

LANDING A KINGFISH, ISLAND-STYLE

In Ernest Hemingway's classic fishing tale, The Old Man and the Sea, an aging fisherman grapples for days with a monstrous marlin. Although I am not an avid fisherman, I have always dreamed of reeling in a really big one and holding it up for the paparazzi to document and photograph.

Well, I didn't actually catch a fish in the Caribbean. After returning from a snorkeling trip one afternoon, I spotted a fishing boat docking nearby. The fisherman tossed a kingfish onto the dock—it had to be at least 5 feet long, maybe longer. While other tourists hurried by, I stood there marveling at this big, beautiful fish. Before anyone knew it, my companion had the camera out and I was holding the prize as if I had just caught it.

At that point, the fisherman asked me if I wanted some steaks cuts from the fish. Right on the dock, he took out a cleaver and sliced off four huge steaks. Instant sushi. Better yet, I carried the steaks back to the hotel (I was reeking of fish, but overcome with delight) and into the restaurant. After a quick introduction to the kitchen staff, I asked if they would prepare it for dinner. They happily obliged. At seven o'clock sharp, we arrived for dinner; the kingfish, lightly marinated in lime, chile peppers, and garlic, soon greeted us. It was one of the tastiest fish dishes I have ever eaten. There was even enough for the kitchen staff to enjoy. The stunt would have amused Hemingway.

Jerk Swordfish and Pineapple Kabobs

Jamaica

Jerk marinade can transform an ordinary barbecue into an adventurous meal. Here it injects a mother lode of flavors to swordfish, pineapple, and grilled vegetables. Serve with Fried Plantains or Pumpkin Rice with Kale.

Marinade

6 green onions, diced
1 medium-size onion, diced
3 to 4 jalapeño or Scotch bonnet peppers, seeded and minced
3/4 cup soy sauce
1/2 cup red wine vinegar
1/4 cup vegetable oil
1/4 cup brown sugar
2 tablespoons fresh thyme leaves
1 teaspoon black peppercorns, crushed
1/2 teaspoon ground cloves
1/2 teaspoon ground nutmeg
1/2 teaspoon ground allspice
1/4 teaspoon ground cinnamon

Kabobs

2 cups cubed fresh pineapple
1 large onion, cut into chunks
1 medium-size red bell pepper, cut into chunks
1 medium-size green pepper, cut into chunks
1 1/2 pounds swordfish steaks, cubed

Combine all of the marinade ingredients in a food processor fitted with a steel blade. Process the mixture for 10 to 15 seconds at high speed. Set aside.

To prepare the fish, skewer alternately the pineapple, onion, peppers, and swordfish cubes, piercing the center of the ingredients. Repeat the process until all of the ingredients are on skewers.

Place the kabobs in a shallow pan and pour the marinade evenly over them. Refrigerate for 4 to 6 hours. Rotate the skewers after 3 hours.

Preheat the grill until the coals are gray to white.

Remove the skewered kabobs from the marinade and drain off any excess liquid. Place on the lightly oiled grill and cook for 5 to 7 minutes on each side, or until the fish is done in the center. Serve the kabobs immediately.

Yield: 4 servings

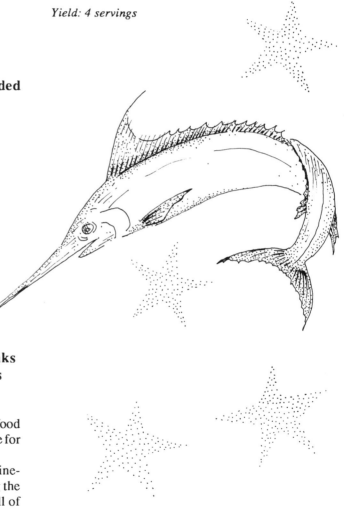

Caribe Steakfish Pie

West Indies

2 tablespoons vegetable oil
1 medium-size onion, diced
2 cloves garlic, minced
1 chile pepper, seeded and minced
2 tablespoons curry powder
1 tablespoon ground cumin
1 teaspoon ground cloves
1/2 teaspoon salt
1/2 teaspoon freshly ground black pepper
2 cups diced pumpkin or sweet potato
2 cups water
1 cup cooked chickpeas
1 pound steakfish (shark, tuna, blue marlin, or swordfish), cubed
Dough for Stuffed Roti (page 86) or Jamaican Beef Patties (page 80)

In a saucepan, place the oil, onion, garlic, and chile pepper and saute for about 5 minutes, until the vegetables are soft. Add the seasonings and cook for 1 minute more, stirring frequently. Add the pumpkin and water and cook for about 15 minutes, stirring occasionally. Stir in the chickpeas and cook for another 5 minutes. Add the fish cubes and cook for 5 minutes more, or until the fish is done in the center. Remove from the heat.

Meanwhile, preheat the oven to 400 degrees.

Divide the dough into 2 even balls. Roll out the balls into 10-inch circles. Place one circle of the dough in a lightly greased 9-inch round cake pan and work the dough up the sides of the pan. Spread the pumpkin and fish mixture over the dough and cover with the remaining circle of dough. Seal the edges with a fork and puncture the top a few times. Place the pie in the oven and bake for 20 to 25 minutes, until the crust is brown. Remove from the oven and allow to cool 5 minutes before serving.

Yield: 6 to 8 servings

Coconut and Lime Grilled Steakfish

West Indies

Steakfish actually refers to any of the many fish that thrive in the Pacific and Caribbean waters—tuna, kingfish, blue marlin, mahimahi, and swordfish, to name a few. Their meat is firm and mildly flavored, making them excellent candidates for marinating and grilling. Coconut and lime impart delicate and subtle flavors to these great catches. For an additional island touch, add 1/4 cup of rum to the marinade.

2 cups coconut milk, fresh or canned, unsweetened
1/4 cup minced fresh cilantro
1/4 cup lime juice
3 jalapeño peppers, seeded and minced
4 cloves garlic, minced
1 tablespoon lime zest
1/2 teaspoon cayenne pepper
1/2 teaspoon ground cloves
1/2 teaspoon ground nutmeg
1/4 teaspoon salt
4 kingfish, tuna, or swordfish steaks, about 8 ounces each
2 teaspoons paprika
1 lime, quartered

Combine the first 10 ingredients in a shallow dish. Place the fish in the marinade and refrigerate for 4 to 6 hours, turning the fish at least once.

Preheat the grill until the coals are gray to white.

Place the fish on the lightly oiled grill and cook for 5 to 7 minutes. Lightly sprinkle 1 teaspoon of the paprika over the steaks. Turn the steaks and continue cooking. Sprinkle the remaining teaspoon of paprika over the steaks. Continue grilling until the fish are cooked in the center. Serve with Mango-Papaya Sauce, Fried Plantains, MoBay Vegetables with Curried Coconut Sauce, or Papaya Mustard Sauce. Garnish with the lime wedges.

Yield: 4 servings

Wok-Seared Tuna with Pineapple Sambal

Pacific Rim

The Chinese tradition of wok cookery is prominent throughout the tropical Pacific Rim. The wok's rapid cooking and even distribution of heat minimize any loss of moisture and flavor. The pineapple sambal can be prepared ahead and served cold or hot.

Sambal

2 cups diced fresh pineapple
1 to 2 chile peppers, seeded and minced
1 cup rice or white wine vinegar
2 cloves garlic, minced
2 tablespoons brown sugar
1 tablespoon soy sauce

Fish

1 tablespoon black peppercorns, crushed
4 tuna steaks, each about 8 ounces
1 lemon, quartered
2 tablespoons vegetable or peanut oil

To make the sambal, combine the pineapple, chile peppers, vinegar, garlic, brown sugar, and soy sauce in a wok or saucepan. Cook over medium heat for 15 to 20 minutes, stirring occasionally. Drain the mixture and discard the liquid. Transfer the sambal to a serving bowl. Serve at once or refrigerate until ready to use.

To prepare the fish, press the peppercorns into the tuna steaks. Squeeze the lemon over the steaks.

Pour the oil into the wok and heat until it is barely smoking. Place the tuna steaks in the wok and cook for 5 to 7 minutes, then turn. Continue cooking until the tuna is cooked in the center. Transfer the fish to warm plates. Spoon some sambal over the steaks and pass the remainder at the table.

Yield: 4 servings

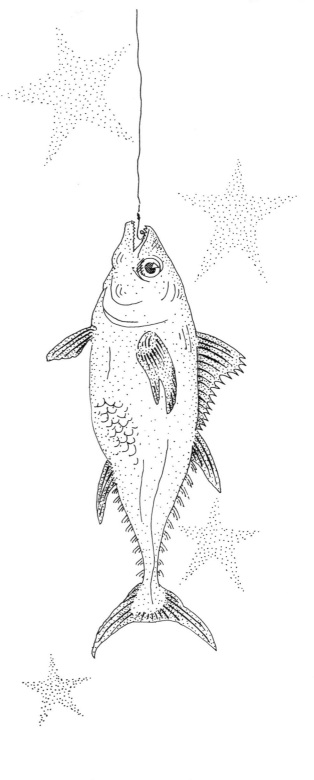

Curried Blue Marlin and Pumpkin Salad

West Indies

This hearty salad combines diverse flavors and textures. Blue marlin, which is plentiful in the Caribbean, is very similar in flavor to tuna. The pumpkin absorbs the fish and curry flavors while adding a tasty nuance of its own.

1 pound blue marlin or tuna steaks
2 cups peeled, diced pumpkin or butternut squash

Curry Mayonnaise

1 egg yolk
1 teaspoon Dijon-style mustard
2 tablespoons lemon juice
3/4 cup olive oil
1 tablespoon minced fresh ginger
2 cloves garlic, minced
1 tablespoon curry powder
1/4 teaspoon ground cloves
1/4 teaspoon turmeric
1/4 teaspoon cayenne pepper
1/4 teaspoon salt

6 to 8 broccoli florets, blanched
1 cup minced celery
1 lemon, quartered

Place the fish steaks in boiling water to cover and cook for 10 minutes, or until the fish is done in the center. Drain and chill under running water. Shred the fish and refrigerate for about 1 hour.

Place the pumpkin in boiling water to cover and cook for 12 minutes, or until it is tender but not mushy. Drain and chill under running water. Refrigerate for about 1 hour.

To make the mayonnaise, blend the egg yolk for 15 seconds in a food processor fitted with a steel blade. Scrape the sides and add the mustard and lemon juice, then process for another 10 seconds. While the motor is running, slowly drizzle in the oil. When half of the oil remains, stop the processor and scrape the sides; then continue processing and drizzling. Add the ginger, garlic, and seasonings and process for another 15 seconds or until all of the ingredients are fully incorporated.

To assemble the salad, combine the curry mayonnaise in a large mixing bowl with the fish, pumpkin, broccoli, and celery. Toss thoroughly. Serve on a bed of lettuce or as a sandwich filling. Before serving, squeeze the lemon over the salad.

Yield: 3 to 4 servings

A FLURRY OF CURRY

The two versions of curry dishes served throughout the tropics are both rooted in Indian cuisine. Curries in the Caribbean islands are an aromatic blend of several spices: turmeric, cumin, coriander, black pepper, cinnamon, fenugreek, cayenne pepper, and cardamom. The curries vary from island to island—some include ginger, garlic, chile peppers, cloves, nutmeg, or dry mustard. Curry was transported to the West Indies (and the New World) by Indian servants indentured by European colonists, and it has thrived ever since.

Thai curries are prepared from a spicy paste of fresh herbs, roots, leaves, and chile peppers. There are several curry pastes: red, green (for red or green chile peppers), yellow or masamun (derived from Indian Muslims), panang, and others. During the cooking process, coconut milk is often added, forming a rich, piquant sauce. The paste can be prepared from scratch or purchased at Asian groceries.

Both types of tropical curries often work their culinary magic in conjunction with garlic, ginger, and hot peppers.

Mahimahi with Papaya Salsa

Hawaii

Mahimahi is Hawaiian for "strong! strong!"—the yell of the Hawaiian fishermen reeling in this fish. In Spanish it is called *dorado*, which means golden, the color of the speckles on their sides. They are also called dolphinfish in English (not to be confused with dolphin, the mammal). Mahimahi is a mild, firmly textured fish ideal for marinating and grilling. The marinade of pineapple juice, soy sauce, and mirin (sweet rice wine) mildly flavors the fish without overpowering it. A salsa made of sweet Hawaiian coral papayas adds a pleasant, palate-cleansing touch to the meal.

Marinade

1/2 cup soy sauce
1/2 cup canned pineapple juice
1/2 cup mirin or sake
2 tablespoons sesame oil
2 tablespoons lime juice
2 tablespoons minced fresh ginger
1 tablespoon minced fresh lemongrass
2 teaspoons red pepper flakes
1 1/2 pounds mahimahi fillets

Salsa

1 ripe papaya, peeled, seeded, and diced
1 chile pepper, seeded and minced
1/4 cup minced red onion
1 clove garlic, minced
Juice of 1 lime
1 tablespoon minced fresh cilantro
1/8 teaspoon salt

To prepare the marinade, combine the soy sauce, pineapple juice, mirin, sesame oil, lime juice, ginger, lemongrass, and red pepper flakes in a shallow glass baking dish. Add the fish and marinate in the refrigerator for 3 to 4 hours. Turn the fillets after 2 hours.

To make the salsa, combine the papaya, chile pepper, red onion, garlic, lime juice, cilantro, and salt in a small mixing bowl.

Set aside.

Preheat the oven to 400 degrees F.

Place the fish in a greased baking pan and pour the excess marinade over the fish. Bake for 12 to 15 minutes, or until the center of the fish is opaque and flakes easily with a fork.

Serve the fish on warm plates and pass the salsa at the table.

Yield: 4 servings

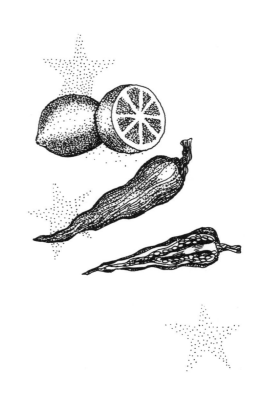

Sea Bass with Banzai! Peanut Sauce

Pacific Rim

Two world-traveling friends of mine, Emily and Jessica, share my penchant for fiery foods. They are often eager to test many of my spicy creations, and the Banzai Peanut Sauce was one of their favorites. The sauce greets your palate with great spirit and vigor, hence the name "Banzai!" In addition to jazzing up pan-fried sea bass or trout, the sauce also lends a nutty, spicy nuance to chicken, pork, lamb, and steamed vegetables.

Sauce

2 tablespoon melted butter or peanut oil
2 to 3 chile peppers, seeded and minced
2 garlic cloves, minced
1/2 cup coconut milk
2 tablespoons unsalted smooth peanut butter
2 tablespoons soy sauce
1 tablespoon lime juice
2 teaspoons sesame oil
1 teaspoon honey
1 teaspoon habañero sauce or your favorite red
   hot sauce

Fish

4 sea bass or trout fillets, about 8 ounces each
1/2 cup all purpose flour
2 tablespoons peanut oil
1 tablespoon minced fresh chives
1 lime, quartered

In a sauce pan, add the melted butter, chile peppers, and garlic and saute for 2 minutes. Stir in the coconut milk, peanut butter, soy sauce, lime juice, sesame oil, honey, and habañero sauce and bring to a simmer. Remove from the heat and set aside.

To prepare the fish, dredge both sides of the fish in the flour. Add the oil to a large skillet and heat until the oil sizzles. Gently place the fish in the pan (flesh side down) and fry over medium heat for 5 to 7 minutes, until the flesh is golden brown. Flip the fish and continue cooking until the fish is cooked in the center. Transfer the fish to warm plates and spoon the peanut sauce over the fish. Sprinkle the chives over the fish, garnish with the lime, and serve immediately.

Yield: 4 servings

Grouper with Creole Eggplant Sauce

St. Martin

Grouper is a mildly flavored, firmly textured fish caught off the shores of many Caribbean islands. I tried grouper for the first time at a restaurant in St. Martin, and the meal was so good that I vowed to re-create it upon my return. Here is a close interpretation of that tasty meal.

Sauce

1/4 cup butter, melted, or vegetable oil
1 cup diced eggplant
1/2 cup diced bell pepper
1/2 cup diced onion
1 tomato, diced
1 clove garlic, minced
1/4 cup canned crushed tomatoes
1/4 cup water
1/2 cup cooked okra, chopped
1 teaspoon dried oregano
1/2 teaspoon red hot sauce
1/4 teaspoon freshly ground black pepper
1/4 teaspoon white pepper
1/8 teaspoon cayenne pepper
1/8 teaspoon red pepper flakes
1/8 teaspoon salt

4 grouper fillets, about 8 ounces each
1/2 cup all-purpose flour
1 lime, quartered

To prepare the sauce, place in a saucepan 2 tablespoons of the butter, plus the eggplant, bell pepper, onion, tomato, and garlic. Saute over medium heat for 6 to 8 minutes, or until the vegetables are soft. Add the crushed tomatoes, water, okra, and seasonings and bring to a simmer. Cook for 5 minutes over low heat, stirring frequently. Set aside.

To cook the fish, place the remaining 2 tablespoons butter in a large, preheated skillet. Dredge the grouper fillets lightly in the flour and place in the skillet. Cook over medium heat for 5 to 7 minutes on each side.

Remove the fillets to warm serving plates and spoon the eggplant sauce over the top. Serve immediately, garnished with the lime wedges.

Yield: 4 servings

PASS THE LIQUID FIRE, PLEASE

Caribbean hot sauces have recently been exploding onto the market. Almost all of them are laced with Scotch bonnet peppers (or habañero peppers). Melinda's Hot Sauce, from Belize, is a carrot-based sauce with several levels of heat. (The XXXtra Hot Sauce, comprised of mostly Scotch bonnets, is one of the hottest and most flavorful sauces I have ever tasted.) Island Style and Helen's Tropical Sauces, derived from Jamaican peppers, are smooth and extremely flavorful.

Matouk's, from Trinidad, is a fruity, papaya-based sauce that emphasizes the fragrant nature of Scotch bonnets with a hint of mustard. Inner Beauty, prepared in Costa Rica, has a curry nuance and is worth buying for the entertaining label alone: "This is serious. This is not a toy." Pickapeppa, another Jamaican concoction, is a sweet-and-spicy version of A-1 Sauce and is a good sauce for beginners.

Many of these condiments are available at specialty food stores or West Indian groceries, or through mail-order sources. Most are great to pour on pizza, hamburgers, chicken wings, scrambled eggs, and any other dish that needs a jolt of fire and spice.

Saltfish and Ackee

Jamaica

Saltfish and ackee is the national dish of Jamaica, but fresh ackee cannot be imported to this country. Fresh ackee is pinkish-yellow with an oblong, mango-like shape. When mature, the fruit bursts open exposing a yellow flesh and black seeds. Ackee—which has the consistency of scrambled eggs—often is served with saltfish at breakfast.

Ackee trees grow throughout Jamaica, but they are rare on most other islands because ackee is considered poisonous if underripe or overripe. If you go to Jamaica, do try this tasty dish, if only for the culinary adventure.

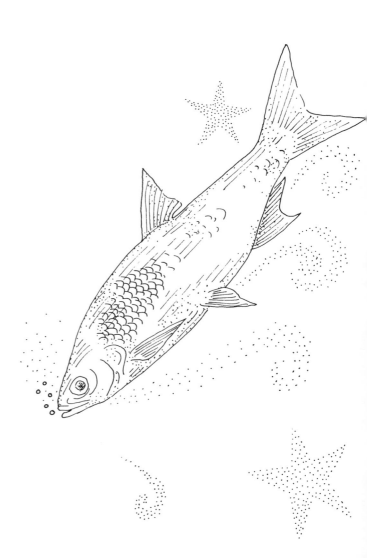

1 pound salted codfish, preferably boned
1/4 pound diced salt pork or 6 bacon strips
1/4 cup coconut or vegetable oil
1 hot pepper, seeded and sliced
2 scallions, chopped
1 medium-size tomato, finely chopped
1 onion, chopped
1 (19-ounce) can ackees
1/2 teaspoon freshly ground black pepper
1 green bell pepper, seeded and chopped

Soak the codfish in cold water to cover for about 30 minutes. Drain and place the fish in 1 quart of water. Bring to a rolling boil, then drain the water. Remove any bones and skin from the codfish and flake the meat with a fork, then set it aside.

Place the salt pork or bacon in a skillet and fry until crisp in its own oil. Reduce the heat and add the coconut oil, hot pepper, scallions, tomato, and onion. Saute until the onion is translucent.

Drain the ackees and stir into the skillet with flaked codfish. Sprinkle with the black pepper, cover, and cook over low heat for 5 minutes. Remove serving portions from the skillet with a slotted spoon to avoid the excess oil. Garnish with the sweet green pepper. Serve with boiled green bananas, roasted breadfruit slices, and dumplings.

This recipe comes from Dunston Harris, *Island Cooking.*

Yield: 4 servings

Plantain-Crusted Grouper

West Indies

Plantains, which are plentiful in the Caribbean, are used to make flour. The plantains are sliced, dried, and ground. In addition to serving as a thickening agent for sauces, plantain flour makes a crunchy and nutritious coating for fish and chicken. Uninitiated guests at my restaurant have a hard time envisioning this dish, but once they taste it, they remember it well.

1/2 cup lime juice
1/4 cup dry white wine
4 grouper fillets, about 8 ounces each
2 green plantains, peeled and sliced thinly
1 tablespoon Island Seasoning (page 25)
2 eggs, beaten
1/4 cup milk
1/4 cup vegetable oil
1 lime, quartered

Combine the lime juice and wine in a shallow bowl. Marinate the grouper in the mixture for 1 to 2 hours.

Preheat the oven to 200 degrees F.

Spread the sliced plantains out on a baking sheet. Bake for 1 1/2 to 2 hours, or until the plantains are dry. Cool the plantains and add them to a food processor fitted with a steel blade. Process for about 30 seconds, to the consistency of coarse flour. Sift the flour and reprocess any large crumbs. Combine the Island Seasoning with the plantain flour and place in a shallow dish.

Combine the eggs with the milk in a shallow bowl. Dunk each fillet in the egg wash, coating both sides, then dredge in the plantain flour, again coating both sides.

In a skillet, place 2 tablespoons of the oil and bring to a sizzle over medium heat. Place 2 fillets in the skillet and cook for 5 to 7 minutes on each side. Repeat the process with the remaining fillets, adding a little more oil if necessary. Serve the fish immediately, garnished with the lime wedges. Tomatillo Hot Sauce, Creole Sauce, or Papaya Mustard Sauce makes a nice condiment.

Yield: 4 servings

Lobster Paella

Philippines

Paella is a hearty rice dish found on many of the Spanish speaking islands in the Caribbean as well as the Philippines. It often is prepared with a combination of shellfish, chicken, fish, and chorizo (Spanish sausage). Saffron, the world's most expensive spice, imparts a golden yellow color to the dish. If saffron is unavailable, try substituting a small amount of turmeric.

12 cups water
2 live lobsters, 1 1/2 pounds each
2 tablespoons butter, melted
1 pound skinless, boneless chicken thighs,
  chopped
1/2 pound chorizo
1 medium-size onion, diced
1 medium-size bell pepper, seeded and diced
1 tomato, diced
2 cloves garlic, minced
1 jalapeño pepper, seeded and minced
2 cups uncooked rice
3 1/2 cups lobster or chicken stock
1/2 cup dry white wine
1 teaspoon saffron threads
1 teaspoon paprika
1/2 teaspoon salt
1/2 teaspoon freshly ground black pepper
1 cup green peas, frozen and thawed

Bring the water to a boil and add the lobsters. Allow the water to return to a boil and cook for 12 minutes, then drain. (Save the water if you are making lobster stock; otherwise discard the water.) Cool the lobster slightly under cold running water. Remove the meat from the lobster tail and claws, picking out cartilage and bones. Set the meat aside.

In a large saucepan, place the butter and the chicken and saute over medium heat. Cook for 7 to 10 minutes. With a slotted spoon, remove the chicken and keep warm.

To the juices in the pan, add the chorizo and cook for about 5 minutes.

Add the onion, bell pepper, tomato, garlic, and jalapeño pepper to the pan and saute for 7 to 10 minutes, or until the vegetables are soft. Add the rice, lobster stock, wine, and seasonings and cover the saucepan. Simmer for 15 minutes, stirring occasionally. Add the lobster meat, chicken, and peas and continue cooking until all of the liquid is absorbed.

Serve the paella with warm bread. For extra pizzazz, spoon Sofrito or Creole Sauce over the top.

Yield: 6 to 8 servings

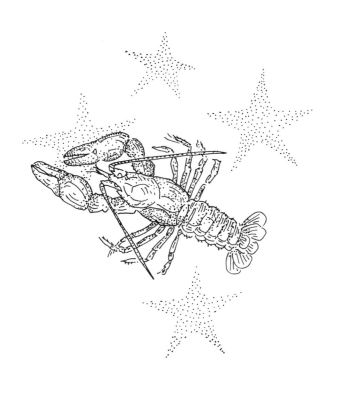

Lobster in Spicy Black Bean Sauce

Spanish West Indies

Black bean sauces and soups are prominent on many of the Hispanic islands in the Caribbean. Black beans offer an earthy flavor and sustenance to the meal and act as an excellent medium for spicy flavors. I enjoy this sauce with lobster, but you can substitute sea scallops or shrimp.

12 cups water
2 live lobsters, 2 pounds each
2 tablespoons butter, melted
1 ripe plantain, peeled and sliced
1 medium-size onion, diced
1 medium-size bell pepper, seeded and diced
2 Scotch bonnet or jalapeño peppers, seeded and minced
1 clove garlic, minced
1 cup cooked black beans
1 cup low-sodium chicken stock or water
1/8 cup red wine
2 teaspoons ground cumin
1/4 teaspoon cayenne pepper
1/4 teaspoon salt
1 cup cooked okra, diced
1 tablespoon minced fresh cilantro

Bring the water to a boil and add the lobsters. Allow the water to return to a boil and cook for 12 minutes, then drain. (Save the water if you are making lobster stock; otherwise, discard the water.) Cool the lobster slightly under cold running water. Remove the meat from the lobster tail and claws, picking out cartilage and bones. Set the meat aside.

In a saucepan, place the butter and plantain slices and cook over medium heat until the plantains are golden brown. Remove them to a warm plate. Add the onion, bell pepper, Scotch bonnet pepper, and garlic to the pan and saute for 7 to 10 minutes, until the vegetables are soft.

Add the black beans, chicken stock, wine, cumin, cayenne, and salt and simmer over medium heat for 15 minutes.

Place the bean mixture in a food processor fitted with a steel blade and process for 15 to 20 seconds. Return the sauce to the pan, along with the lobster meat, plantains, okra, and cilantro. Bring the mixture to a simmer, stirring frequently. Serve steaming hot over rice.

Yield: 4 servings

SPINY LOBSTERS

Spiny lobsters are cousins of North American lobsters and crawfish, and can be found in the Pacific and Caribbean waters. Spiny lobsters, however, are a bit narrower and lack the ominous large claws of their North American relatives. Also known as langouste or langosta in the Caribbean, the spiny lobster is prized for the meat in its tail. The usual way to cook it is to boil it in a highly seasoned water bath. Maine lobsters may be substituted for spiny lobsters in most recipes.

Stir-Fried Mussels and Noodles

Pacific Rim

4 dozen mussels
4 ounces rice noodles
1 teaspoon cornstarch
1 teaspoon water
2 tablespoons peanut or vegetable oil
2 cloves garlic, minced
1 chile pepper, seeded and minced
2 teaspoons minced fresh ginger
1 cup coconut milk, fresh or canned, unsweetened
2 tablespoons soy sauce or fish sauce
1 tablespoon lime juice
1 tablespoon peanut butter
1/2 teaspoon laos (available where Asian foods
   are sold), optional
2 tablespoons minced fresh basil or 1 tablespoon
   minced fresh cilantro

Scrub the mussels and remove the beards. Discard any mussels that are already open. In a large pot, bring about 2 inches of water to a boil. Place a colander over the pot, add the mussels, and cover. Steam for 5 to 7 minutes, until the mussels open. Transfer the mussels to a plate and discard any that did not open. Remove the meat and discard the shells.

Place the rice noodles in a pot of boiling water and cook for 6 to 8 minutes, until al dente. Drain the noodles in a colander. In a small bowl, combine the cornstarch and water and set aside.

In a wok, heat the oil and add the garlic, chile pepper, and ginger. Stir-fry for 2 to 3 minutes. Add the coconut milk, soy sauce, lime juice, peanut butter, and laos and bring to a simmer. Stir the cornstarch paste into the mixture in the wok. Add the steamed mussels, cooked noodles, and basil and bring to a simmer, stirring frequently. Serve immediately on warm plates.

Yield: 4 servings

Volcano Scallops with Thai Curry Sauce

Thailand

Let's face it: We all have vices, whether its procrastinating, watching soap operas, reading trashy novels, indulging in rich desserts, and so forth. My vice is eating extremely spicy meals, pushing the lid back on the stratosphere of heat, and discovering new dimensions of fiery food. This meal exemplifies my passion for nose-tingling, eye-watering, lip-numbing meals. Of course, this meal can tempered by reducing the chile peppers and green curry paste. And omit the "volcano" when referring to it. That's allowed.

1 teaspoon cornstarch
1 teaspoon water
2 tablespoons peanut oil
1 pound sea scallops
2 teaspoons minced fresh lemongrass
2 teaspoons minced fresh ginger
2 to 3 chile peppers, minced
2 cloves garlic, minced
2 teaspoons green curry paste
1 cup coconut milk, fresh or canned, unsweetened
3 tablespoons soy sauce
1 cup bok choy
6 to 8 broccoli florets

In a small mixing bowl, combine the cornstarch and water and set aside.

Heat the oil in a wok until it sizzles, coating the sides. Add the scallops to the wok and cook for about 7 minutes, until the centers of the scallops are clear and white. Stir occasionally. Remove to a warm plate.

Add the lemongrass, ginger, chile peppers, garlic, and green curry paste to the wok and cook for 2 to 3 minutes, stirring frequently. Add the coconut milk and soy sauce and bring to a simmer. Stir in the scallops, bok choy, broccoli, and cornstarch mixture. Simmer for 2 to 3 minutes. Serve over rice.

Yield: 3 to 4 servings

Scallops with Curried Chickpea Sauce

West Indies

When two or three ingredients are combined, the whole often is tastier than the sum of the parts. The triumvirate of curry powder, chickpeas, and sweet potatoes perfectly illustrates this principle. In my kitchen, these flavors have become as revered as the other two famous trios of tomato, basil, and garlic, and cilantro, jalapeno pepper, and lime juice. The curry sauce is warm, filling, and versatile; it's delicious with shellfish, chicken, or pork.

Sauce

2 tablespoons butter, melted
1 medium-size red onion, diced
1 medium-size red bell pepper, finely chopped
2 cloves garlic, minced
1 Scotch bonnet pepper or jalapeño pepper, seeded
  and minced
2 teaspoons minced fresh ginger
2 tablespoons curry powder
1 teaspoon ground cumin
1/2 teaspoon ground cloves
1/2 teaspoon freshly ground black pepper
1/4 teaspoon salt
2 sweet potatoes, scrubbed and chopped
2 cups water
2 cups cooked chickpeas

2 tablespoons butter, melted
2 pounds sea scallops, washed
1 cup cooked okra, chopped

To make the sauce, place the melted butter, red onion, bell pepper, garlic, Scotch bonnet pepper, and ginger in a deep skillet and saute for 5 to 6 minutes over medium heat. Add the curry powder, cumin, cloves, black pepper, and salt and saute for another 2 minutes. Add the potatoes and water and simmer for about 15 minutes, or until the potatoes are soft. Lower the heat, add the chickpeas, and cook for another 10 minutes, or until the sauce is thick and chunky. Set the sauce aside.

In a large skillet, place the melted butter and scallops. Saute over moderately high heat for 10 to 12 minutes. Add the okra and cook for another 2 minutes. Add the chickpea sauce. Simmer for 4 to 5 minutes, stirring frequently. Serve the curried scallops with Pumpkin Rice and Kale or rice.

Yield: 4 servings

Shrimp and Crab Pilau

West Indies

Pilau is a hearty rice dish prepared in the same spirit as the Creole dish jambalaya and the Spanish paella. The curry and coconut flavors simmer with the rice and the seafood, and the result is a rewarding, mouth-watering feast.

1/4 cup butter, melted
1 medium-size onion, minced
3 cloves garlic, minced
1 Scotch bonnet pepper, seeded and minced
1 tomato, diced
2 tablespoons curry powder
1/2 teaspoon freshly ground black pepper
1/2 teaspoon salt
1 1/2 cups uncooked rice
3 1/2 cups coconut milk, fresh or canned, unsweetened
1/2 pound crabmeat
16 to 20 large shrimp, peeled and deveined
1 cup cooked pigeon peas or kidney beans

Place the butter in a saucepan and add the onion, garlic, bonnet pepper, and tomato. Saute for 5 to 7 minutes. Add the curry powder, black pepper, and salt and saute for another 2 minutes. Stir in the rice and cook for another 2 minutes, making sure to coat the rice with the curry mixture. Add the coconut milk and cook for over low heat for 20 minutes.

Add the crabmeat, shrimp, and pigeon peas. Reduce the heat and cook for another 5 to 10 minutes, or until the rice has absorbed all of the liquid and the shrimp is firm and pink. Stir occasionally. Serve immediately with warm bread.

Yield: 4 servings

Shrimp and Mango Curry

West Indies

Curry powder reached the West Indies via India, and it has become a major seasoning of Caribbean cuisine. Curry is a blend of seasonings, often consisting of turmeric, coriander, cumin, cinnamon, ginger, fenugreek, dry mustard, peppercorns, pepper flakes, and cayenne. Storebought curries vary in degree of spiciness, but they are easy to adjust by adding cayenne and turmeric for more heat, or cumin and cinnamon for less. Curry dishes frequently include garlic, ginger, and hot peppers. It's an ideal seasoning for this dish of shrimp, mangoes, and potatoes.

2 tablespoons butter, melted
6 green onions, minced
2 cloves garlic, minced
1 tablespoon minced fresh ginger
2 tablespoons curry powder
1/8 teaspoon cayenne pepper
1/4 teaspoon salt
1 large sweet potato, scrubbed and diced
1 1/2 cups water
16 large shrimp, peeled and deveined
1 mango, peeled, pitted, and diced

Place the butter in a saucepan and saute the green onions, garlic, and ginger for 3 minutes. Add the curry powder, cayenne, and salt and saute for another 2 minutes. Add the sweet potato and water and cook over medium heat for 15 minutes. Add the shrimp and mango and cook for 5 to 7 minutes more, stirring occasionally. Serve immediately.

Yield: 2 servings

Tropical Crepe with Chevre and Shrimp

Indonesia

Crepe Batter

3 eggs, beaten
1 1/2 cups all-purpose flour
1 1/2 cups milk
1/4 teaspoon salt
1/8 teaspoon freshly ground pepper
1/4 cup plus 2 tablespoons melted butter
1 cup shredded bok choy or spinach
3 tablespoons butter

Filling

12 broccoli florets
2 tablespoons butter
20 to 26 small shrimp, peeled and deveined
8 mushrooms, sliced
1 red bell pepper, seeded and minced
2 tablespoons minced shallots
1 tablespoon minced fresh lemongrass
1 tablespoon minced fresh ginger
10 to 12 ounces chevre, chopped coarsely

To make the crepes, combine the eggs, flour, milk, salt, and pepper in a large mixing bowl. Fold in the melted butter and bok choy and refrigerate for 1 hour.

Melt 1 tablespoon of the butter in an 8-inch crepe pan or skillet and ladle about 1/2 cup of batter into the pan. Tilt the pan to ease the batter around the base of the pan and form a thin, round pancake. When the edges of the crepe are light brown, flip the crepe with a smooth motion. Continue cooking until the surface is light brown, then remove to a warm plate.

Cook the remaining batter in the same fashion, adding about 1 teaspoon of butter to the pan after cooking each crepe. Stack the crepes on a warm plate, placing a sheet of waxed paper between each one. Cover the stack.

To make the filling, blanch the broccoli in boiling water to cover for 3 minutes. Drain and chill under cold running water. Melt the butter over moderately high heat in a large skillet. Add the shrimp, broccoli, mushrooms, bell pepper, shallots, lemongrass, and ginger and cook for 6 to 8 minutes, or until the shrimp are firm and light pink. Stir the mixture occasionally.

Reduce the heat to low and stir the chevre into the mixture. When the cheese is fully incorporated, remove the pan from the heat.

Place a crepe on each of 4 warmed dinner plates. Spoon one-fourth of the filling on each, lengthwise down in the middle. Roll the crepe around the filling and serve immediately with salsa or chutney.

Yield: 4 servings

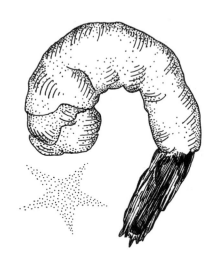

Shrimp, Mango and Pineapple Stir-Fry

Indonesia

I frequently add mangoes and pineapples to stir-fries because of their tendency to absorb the strong soy flavors while maintaining a zesty, distinct presence of their own. They also provide contrasting textures, colors, and nutrients.

3 tablespoons soy sauce
2 tablespoons butter, melted
1 tablespoon lime juice
2 teaspoons minced fresh ginger
2 cloves garlic, minced
1/2 teaspoon red hot sauce
1 bell pepper, seeded and diced
1 cup unpeeled, diced eggplant
1 cup diced fresh pineapple
1 cup peeled, pitted, and diced mango
16 medium-size shrimp, peeled and deveined
3 cups cooked jasmine or white rice

Place 2 tablespoons of the soy sauce, plus the butter, lime juice, ginger, garlic, and red hot sauce in a large skillet or wok. Cook over medium heat for 1 minute, then add the bell pepper, eggplant, pineapple, mango, and shrimp. Saute for 6 to 8 minutes, or until the shrimp are white and firm in the center. Stir in the rice and remaining soy sauce and cook for another 3 to 5 minutes, or until the rice is steaming. Serve immediately.

Yield: 2 servings

Poultry, Beef, Pork, & Lamb

Island-Roasted Chicken with Thyme Mustard Sauce

West Indies

Caribbean street markets display bunches and bunches of thyme, tucked among mangoes, papayas, and Scotch bonnet peppers. Thyme's warm, pungent aroma balances the sweet spices—nutmeg, allspice, clove, and cinnamon—and complements the sharpness of mustard. I developed this recipe for a story on thyme for *The Herb Companion*.

Seasoning Mixture

1/2 teaspoon ground allspice
1/2 teaspoon ground nutmeg
1/2 teaspoon ground cloves
1/2 teaspoon ground cinnamon
1/2 teaspoon cayenne pepper
1/4 teaspoon salt

1 tablespoon butter, softened
1 whole chicken, about 3 to 4 pounds, washed and
  patted dry
6 to 8 cloves garlic, slivered
1/2 tablespoon whole cloves
10 to 12 stems fresh thyme, 4 to 6 inches long
1 cup Thyme Mustard Sauce, warmed

Preheat the oven to 375 degrees F.

Combine the seasoning mixture in a small bowl and set aside. Spread the butter evenly over the chicken and in the cavity. Insert the garlic and cloves under the skin, over the breasts and drumsticks, and inside the cavity. Sprinkle the seasoning mixture over the chicken, under the skin, and inside the cavity. Stuff the thyme stems in the cavity and underneath the skin.

Place the chicken on a rack in a roasting pan and roast for about 75 minutes, or until a leg can be easily twisted. Baste every 15 minutes with the pan juices.

Remove the chicken from the pan and place it on a serving platter. Garnish with the thyme stems and garlic, forming a crown around the chicken. Pass the Thyme Mustard Sauce at the table.

Yield: 3 to 4 servings

THYME MUSTARD SAUCE

3/4 cup light or heavy cream
1/4 cup Dijon-style mustard
3 tablespoons fresh thyme leaves
1/8 teaspoon white pepper

Combine all of the ingredients in a small bowl. Just before serving, warm the mustard sauce in a microwave until it simmers, or place it in the top of a double boiler and bring it to the desired temperature. Serve with Island-Roasted Chicken. This also makes an appropriate condiment for fish, beef, or pork entrees.

Yield: 1 cup

Colombo and Banana-Roasted Chicken

French West Indies

Colombo refers to the curry mixture of spices found on the French-speaking islands of the West Indies. The tangy banana paste in this recipe infuses the chicken with a strong curry flavor and a fruity nuance. When this is baking in the oven, the whole kitchen will have a banana-bread aroma.

2 bananas, peeled and chopped
2 tablespoons curry powder
1 tablespoon ground cumin
1 teaspoon ground coriander
1 teaspoon turmeric
1 teaspoon dry mustard
1 teaspoon ground cloves
1 teaspoon freshly ground black pepper
1/2 teaspoon salt
2 tablespoons butter, softened
1 whole chicken, about 3 pounds

Preheat the oven to 375 degrees F.

Place all of the ingredients, except the chicken, in a food processor fitted with a steel blade. Process for 15 to 20 seconds, forming a paste.

Rub the chicken with the banana paste; force the paste underneath the skin, into the cavity, and into any crevices.

Place the chicken in a baking pan and roast for 45 minutes to 1 hour. Baste with the pan juices every 15 minutes.

Remove the chicken from the oven and cover with aluminum foil. Allow to stand for about 10 minutes before carving.

Serve the chicken with Mango Chutney, Tropical Fruit Chutney, Apricot-Fig Relish, or Papaya Mustard Sauce.

Yield: 4 servings

Pirated Chicken

West Indies

The tropics are filled with legends of buried treasures, rum-chugging pirates, mutinies, and mysterious shipwrecks. This recipe has a treasure trove of flavor, and, like a pirate ship, it is filled with ingredients from a variety of islands.

1 whole chicken, about 3 to 4 pounds
1/2 cup soy sauce
1/2 cup dark rum
1/4 cup vegetable oil
1/4 cup lime juice
1 medium-size onion
1 1/2 tablespoons minced fresh ginger
3 to 4 cloves garlic, minced
2 to 3 chile peppers, seeded and minced
1/4 cup fresh thyme leaves
2 tablespoons minced fresh parsley
1/2 teaspoon dry mustard
2 teaspoons cornstarch
2 teaspoons water

Cut the chicken into halves, clip the wings, and remove the excess bones around the chicken breast. Place all of the chicken sections in a roasting pan.

Place the remaining ingredients, except the cornstarch and water, in a food processor fitted with a steel blade. Process for 15 seconds, forming a mash. Pour the mash over the chicken and refrigerate for 2 hours.

Preheat the oven to 350 degrees F.

Place the chicken in the oven and bake for 45 minutes to 1 hour, until the meat pulls easily from the bone. Baste the chicken with the pan juices every 20 minutes and turn the chicken sections at least once.

Combine the cornstarch and water and set aside.

Transfer the chicken to serving plates. In a skillet, place the mash and the pan juices. Add the cornstarch mixture and bring to a simmer over medium heat, stirring occasionally. Ladle the sauce into a serving bowl and pass it at the table.

Yield: 4 servings

Chicken and Plantains with Mango Chutney

West Indies

Chutney is a sweet-and-tart condiment prepared with a variety of fruits, such as pineapples, papayas, apples, peaches, and of course mangoes. Mango chutney is an Indian and British legacy in the Caribbean. Although chutneys traditionally were served on the side, as with a relish, I have developed chutneys that make bold, hearty sauces. In addition, chutneys have no cholesterol or fat, and negligible salt.

2 tablespoons butter, melted
1 ripe plantain, peeled and sliced
1 pound skinless, boneless, chicken breasts, cut into strips
1 cup diced cooked okra

Mango Chutney

2 mangoes, peeled, pitted, and chopped
3/4 cup diced onion
1/2 cup diced apple or pear
1/2 cup brown sugar
1/2 cup red wine vinegar
1 Scotch bonnet or jalapeño pepper, seeded
   and minced
1 tablespoon minced fresh ginger
3 to 4 cloves garlic, minced
1/2 teaspoon ground cumin
1/4 teaspoon ground cloves
1/4 teaspoon salt
1/8 teaspoon cayenne pepper

Place the butter and plantains in a large skillet. Cook over medium heat for 7 to 10 minutes, or until the plantain slices are golden brown on both sides. Remove the plantain from the skillet and add the chicken strips. Saute the chicken strips until the centers are white.

Combine all of the chutney ingredients in a large, nonreactive saucepan and cook over low heat, stirring occasionally. Simmer for 15 to 20 minutes, until the mixture has a jamlike consistency. Allow the chutney to cool to room temperature.

Return the plantains to the skillet and add the okra and cooled chutney. Bring the mixture to a simmer and cook for 2 to 3 minutes, stirring occasionally. Serve with rice.

The chutney can be made ahead of time, and will keep for several weeks if refrigerated.

Yield: 2 servings

Grilled Chicken with Peanut Sauce

Tahiti

1/4 cup peanut or vegetable oil
1/4 cup soy sauce
1/4 cup cilantro leaves
2 cloves garlic
2 chile peppers, seeded and minced
2 tablespoons peanut butter
1 tablespoon minced fresh lemongrass
1 tablespoon lime juice
1 tablespoon ground coriander
1 tablespoon ground cumin
1 1/2 pounds skinless, boneless chicken breasts, pounded thin

Place all of the ingredients, except the chicken, in a food processor fitted with a steel blade. Process for 30 seconds, until the mixture forms a paste. Place the chicken in a bowl and pour the marinade over it. Refrigerate for 4 hours or overnight.

Preheat the grill until the coals are gray to white.

Remove the chicken from the marinade and place on the lightly oiled grill. Cook for 4 to 5 minutes on each side, or until the chicken is white in the center. Serve over rice with Indonesian Peanut Sauce.

Yield: 3 to 4 servings

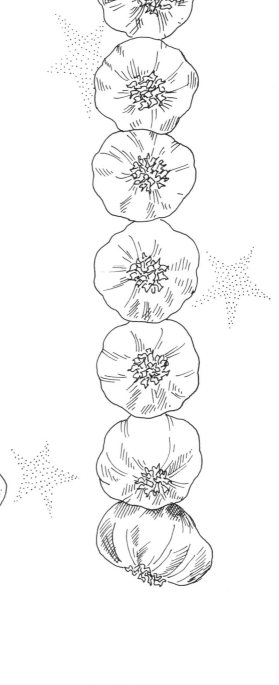

Jerk Chicken

Jamaica

When I began offering Jerk chicken at my restaurant, it quickly became the rage among the customers. I soon changed my restaurant slogan to "Ithaca's home for Jerk barbecue." Jerk cooking is a Jamaican method of marinating, seasoning, and barbecuing chicken, pork, or beef, usually in jerk pits alongside the bumpy roads of Jamaica. The marinade is sweet, hot, and very spicy, and full of complex flavors.

6 to 8 green onions, diced
1 medium-size onion, diced
2 to 4 Scotch bonnet peppers or jalapeño peppers, seeded and minced
3/4 cup soy sauce
1/2 cup red wine vinegar
1/4 cup vegetable oil
1/4 cup brown sugar
2 tablespoons fresh thyme leaves
1 teaspoon whole cloves, crushed
1 teaspoon black peppercorns, crushed
1/2 teaspoon ground cloves
1/2 teaspoon ground nutmeg
1/2 teaspoon ground allspice
1/4 teaspoon ground cinnamon
1 1/2 pounds skinless, boneless chicken breast, cut into strips

Place all of the ingredients, except the chicken, in a food processor fitted with a steel blade. Process for 10 to 15 seconds at high speed. Place the chicken in a bowl and pour the marinade over it. Refrigerate for 4 to 6 hours.

Preheat the grill until the coals are gray to white.

Remove the chicken from the marinade and drain off any excess liquid. Place on the oiled grill and cook for 4 to 5 minutes on each side, or until the chicken is white in the center. Serve the chicken with Fried Plantains, Pumpkin Rice with Kale, and steamed okra.

Yield: 4 servings

Variation

Jerk chicken can also be baked in the oven. Pour the jerk marinade over 4 chicken drumsticks and 4 chicken thighs and refrigerate for 4 to 6 hours, turning after 3 hours. Remove the chicken pieces from the marinade and place on a baking sheet. Bake at 375 degrees for 45 minutes to 1 hour, or until the meat pulls easily away from the bone.

THE SAGA OF JERK BARBECUE

Jerk barbecue is the Jamaican way of marinating and grilling chicken, pork, and fish. Throughout the island, jerk huts line the roadsides. Scotch bonnet peppers—along with thyme, green onions, nutmeg, cloves, and allspice—provide the fuel for the jerk sauce. Like the American barbecue, every jerk pit claims to use a slightly different—and superior—recipe.

The jerk method of slowly basting and cooking highly seasoned meat is credited to the Jamaican Maroons, runaway slaves escaped from the British in the 1600s. The Maroons preserved and cooked the pork in deep pits and basted it with herbs, spices, and chile peppers. Jerk shacks eventually sprang up everywhere.

The term jerk is thought to be derived from the Spanish word charqui, which means dried meat. (In English, this became the beef jerky.) Another story goes that the pork was jerked from side to side on the grill as it cooked—hence the name jerked pork. The cook was known as a jerk man or jerk woman.

A trip to Jamaica is not complete unless you've visited a local jerk center. Using a cleaver, the jerk man hacks the jerked meat into small pieces and piles them high in a basket. Additional jerk sauce can be spooned over the meat. Roasted breadfruit, yams, and Red Stripe beer are also on the menu at jerk huts.

Chicken Satay

Indonesia

Satays are the backyard barbecue of Southeast Asia. Like American barbecue sauces, there are many satay marinades and sauces. Most of the satays include soy or fish sauce, lime juice, peanut butter, coconut milk, vinegar, lemongrass, and chile peppers or pastes. Everything from lamb and fish to beef, pork, and chicken can be used for a satay. Indonesian Peanut Sauce makes an excellent accompaniment to this meal.

2 cups coconut milk, fresh or canned, unsweetened
1/4 cup rice wine vinegar
1 fresh lemongrass stalk, minced, or 1 tablespoon
   lime zest
2 tablespoons chile-garlic paste (available where
   Asian foods are sold)
1 1/2 tablespoons minced fresh cilantro
1 pound skinless, boneless chicken breasts,
   pounded and cut into 2-inch-wide strips

Combine the coconut milk, vinegar, lemongrass, chili paste, and cilantro in a mixing bowl.

Thread the chicken strips onto 10-inch-long metal or bamboo skewers and place in a rectangular casserole dish. Pour the marinade over the skewers and refrigerate for 2 to 3 hours. Turn the skewers after 1 hour.

Preheat the grill until the coals are gray to white.

When the coals are ready, place the skewers on the grill. Turn the skewers occasionally and cook for 7 to 10 minutes or until the chicken is white in the center.

Remove the skewers to warm plates and serve immediately.

Yield: 3 to 4 servings

Curried Chicken with Chickpeas

Trinidad

1/4 cup butter, melted
2 cloves garlic, minced
2 teaspoons minced fresh ginger
1 small onion, diced
2 tablespoons curry powder
2 teaspoons ground cumin
1 teaspoon ground thyme
2 sweet potatoes, scrubbed and diced
1 1/2 cups water
1/2 teaspoon red hot sauce
1/8 teaspoon salt
2 cups cooked chickpeas
1 1/2 pounds skinless, boneless chicken breasts,
   pounded and diced

Place 2 tablespoons of the butter, plus the garlic, ginger, and onion in a deep skillet. Saute for 2 to 3 minutes over medium heat. Add the curry powder, cumin, and thyme and saute for another minute. Add the potatoes, water, red hot sauce, and salt and cook for about 15 minutes, or until the potatoes are soft but not mushy. Add the chickpeas and cook for another 5 to 10 minutes.

In a separate skillet, saute 2 tablespoons of the remaining butter and the chicken over medium heat for 5 to 7 minutes, or until the chicken is white in the center. Add the vegetable curry mixture and bring to a simmer. Serve over hot rice.

Yield: 4 servings

Rum-Soaked Bajan Chicken

Barbados

Barbados is home to miles of public beaches, as well as fertile soil cultivated primarily for sugar cane. Papaya, coconut, mango, and breadfruit trees provide fruit for local consumption. Rum is distilled on the island, and pina coladas and rum desserts abound. Rum also makes a pungent marinade, especially when combined with Bajan seasonings.

1 cup dark rum
1/2 cup lime juice
1/4 cup vegetable oil
2 medium-size red onions, diced
8 green onions, diced
1 to 3 Scotch bonnet peppers or jalapeño peppers,
** seeded and minced**
4 to 5 cloves garlic, minced
2 tablespoons fresh thyme leaves
2 tablespoons minced fresh parsley
2 teaspoons Island Seasoning (page 25)
2 teaspoons red hot sauce
1/2 teaspoon freshly ground black pepper
1/4 teaspoon salt
2 pounds skinless, boneless chicken breasts, cut
** onto strips**
1 teaspoon paprika

Combine the rum, lime juice, oil, red and green onions, peppers, garlic, thyme, parsley, Island Seasonings, red hot sauce, black pepper, and salt in a food processor fitted with a steel blade. Process for 15 to 20 seconds. Pour the mixture into a bowl, add the chicken, and refrigerate for 4 to 6 hours.

Preheat the grill until the coals are gray to white.

Remove the chicken from the marinade and drain off any excess liquid. Place on the lightly oiled grill and cook for 4 to 5 minutes on each side, until the chicken is done in the center. Serve with Black Bean Soup or Sweet Plantain and Saffron-Scented Soup.

Yield: 4 servings

Lemongrass Chicken with Asian Pears

Pacific Rim

Asian pears have the texture of an apple and the sweetness of a pear. This dish grew out of my penchant for combining fruit with main entrees, especially mildly flavored chicken and pork dishes. If Asian pears are unavailable, substitute apples, pears, or firm nectarines.

8 ounces uncooked rice noodles
2 tablespoons butter
1 1/2 pounds skinless, boneless chicken breasts, diced
2 Asian pears, sliced (do not peel)
1 1/4 cups raw, unsalted cashews
1 tablespoon minced fresh lemongrass
1 3/4 cups light cream
1/2 cup Dijon-style mustard

Place the noodles in hot water to cover for 5 minutes, then drain the noodles in a colander and cool under running water.

In a large skillet, melt the butter over medium heat and add the diced chicken breasts. Cook for 4 to 5 minutes, stirring occasionally.

Add the Asian pears and continue to cook for 2 to 3 minutes more, or until the pears are soft and the chicken is white in the center. Add the cashews and lemongrass and cook for 2 minutes more, stirring frequently.

Stir the cream and mustard into the pan and bring the mixture to a simmer. Simmer for about 1 minute more, then blend the noodles thoroughly into the mixture. Cook for about 1 minute more, or until the noodles are steaming.

Transfer to warm plates and serve immediately.

Yield: 4 to 5 servings

Aromatic Chicken with Jackfruit

Java

Jackfruit is a big, lumpy fruit frequently cooked with chicken in Java. It has a mild flavor and adds substance and texture to a meal. The fragrant mixture of lemongrass, shallots, cumin, coriander, and laos create an easy and delectable meal.

Jackfruit is available canned at Asian markets. Dried jackfruit is available through Frieda's Finest but it is not intended for recipes (it's consumed like dried fruit). You can substitute red potatoes or any crunchy vegetables for jackfruit in this recipe. Kaffir lime leaves (dried) are available at Asian grocers.

4 shallots
2 cloves garlic
1 tablespoon minced fresh lemongrass
1/2 cup macadamia or cashew nuts
2 1/2 tablespoons butter
1 1/2 pounds skinless, boneless, chicken breasts, diced
1 cup coconut milk, fresh or canned, unsweetened
1 cup canned jackfruit, diced
1/2 teaspoon ground laos (available where Asian foods are sold) or dried ginger
1/2 teaspoon ground cumin
1/4 teaspoon ground coriander
4 Kaffir lime leaves (available where Asian foods are sold) or 1 teaspoon lime zest

Place the shallots, garlic, lemongrass, and nuts in a food processor fitted with a steel blade. Process for 15 to 20 seconds, forming a paste. Set aside.

Melt the butter in a large skillet. Add the chicken and saute for 5 to 7 minutes, until the chicken is done in the center. Remove the chicken to a warm plate.

Add the nut paste to the skillet and saute for about 2 minutes. Add the coconut milk, jackfruit, seasonings, and lime leaves and bring to a simmer. Return the chicken to the skillet and cook for 4 to 5 minutes, stirring occasionally. Spoon the mixture over rice and remove the lime leaves. Serve immediately.

Yield: 4 servings

Chicharrones de Pollo

Spanish West Indies

These tasty chicken nuggets are the Caribbean version of Kentucky Fried Chicken. They are marinated in rum, lime juice, soy sauce, and spices, then floured and fried. The result is a delectable treat ideal as an appetizer, lunch, or finger-licking dinner. Serve with Mango-Papaya Sauce, Tomatillo Hot Sauce, and/or Papaya Mustard Sauce.

1/2 cup soy sauce
1/2 cup dark rum
1/2 cup lime juice
2 teaspoons paprika
1 teaspoon freshly ground black pepper
2 pounds skinless, boneless chicken thighs
1/2 cup all-purpose flour
2 cups vegetable oil for frying

Combine the soy sauce, rum, lime juice, paprika, and black pepper in a mixing bowl. Add the chicken and marinate for 2 to 4 hours.

Remove the chicken from the marinade, shake off the excess liquid, and pat dry with a paper towel.

Heat the oil in a heavy saucepan until it reaches 375 degrees F.

Dredge the chicken lightly in the flour. Lower the chicken pieces gently into the oil and fry until they are golden brown and cooked in the center. With a slotted spoon, remove the chicken from the oil and drain on paper towels. Serve immediately.

Yield: 4 servings

Gabrielle Roasted Chicken

St. Martin

One of the many adventures I had during my Caribbean vacations was a short voyage to a deserted island. *Gabrielle* was the name of the ship that carried about twenty would-be world-class snorkelers and sun worshippers to a quiet island near St. Martin. The crew prepared lunch while underway. The ship anchored about 50 yards off the coast, and rafts took the passengers onto the pristine beaches. This chicken was our lunch that day, and I extracted the marinade secrets from the crew.

1 cup soy sauce
1/2 cup dark rum
1/2 cup red wine vinegar
1/2 cup vegetable oil
2 tablespoons thyme leaves
1 tablespoon minced fresh ginger
4 to 6 cloves garlic, minced
1 teaspoon freshly ground black pepper
Juice of 1 lime
8 chicken thighs

Combine the soy sauce, rum, vinegar, oil, thyme, ginger, garlic, black pepper, and lime juice in a bowl. Add the chicken thighs and refrigerate for 4 hours. Turn the chicken after 2 hours.

Preheat the oven to 375 degrees F.

Remove the chicken from the marinade with a slotted spoon and place in a baking pan in a single layer. Bake for 45 minutes, or until the meat pulls away easily from the bone. Baste with pan juices every 15 minutes. Serve immediately.

Yield: 4 servings

Bajan Baked Chicken

Barbados

"Chopped seasoning" is a popular blend of spices on the Caribbean island of Barbados. Bajans, as the residents are known, use the blend of seasonings to marinate chicken, fish (especially fried flying fish), and pork.

10 green onions, chopped
1 medium-size onion, diced
1 bell pepper, seeded and diced
1 Scotch bonnet pepper or jalapeño pepper, seeded and minced
3 to 4 cloves garlic, minced
2 tablespoons butter, softened
1 tablespoon fresh thyme leaves
1 tablespoon minced fresh parsley
1/4 cup lime juice
1/4 teaspoon salt
1/4 teaspoon freshly ground pepper
4 chicken thighs
4 chicken drumsticks

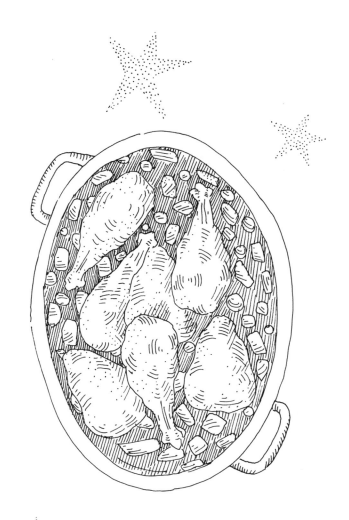

In a food processor fitted with a steel blade, place all of the ingredients except the chicken. Process for 30 seconds, forming a paste. Scrape the sides at least once during the processing. Place the chicken in a bowl, covering it with the paste. Force the paste into any crevices in the chicken. Marinate for 4 to 6 hours.

Preheat the oven to 375 degrees F.

Place the chicken in a baking dish in a single layer and bake for 45 minutes, until the meat pulls easily from the bone. Turn the chicken after 20 minutes and baste with the pan juices. Serve with Pumpkin Rice with Kale or MoBay Vegetables with Curried Coconut Sauce.

Yield: 4 servings

Asopao with Black Beans

Puerto Rico

Asopao is a soupy rice dish similar to paella. For a twist, I've added black beans to the traditional recipe to give it additional texture and flavor. I like to prepare a double batch and reheat the leftovers the next day.

2 tablespoons vegetable oil
4 chicken drumsticks
4 chicken thighs
2 cloves garlic, minced
1 medium-size onion, finely chopped
1 medium-size bell pepper, seeded and finely
   chopped
2 tomatoes, diced
1/2 pound cooked ham, diced
1 1/2 cups uncooked long grain rice
3 cups low sodium chicken stock
1 teaspoon freshly ground black pepper
1 teaspoon dried oregano
1/2 teaspoon salt
1 cup cooked peas
1 cup cooked black beans
1/4 cup grated Parmesan cheese
1 tablespoon capers, drained

Heat the oil in a large skillet over medium heat. Add the chicken pieces and cook for 5 minutes, turning occasionally to brown all sides. (You may pull off the skin and discard it.)

Remove the chicken from the skillet. Add the garlic, onion, bell pepper, and tomatoes and saute for 5 minutes. Return the chicken to the pan and add the ham. Cover the pan and cook for 30 minutes, turning the chicken occasionally. Remove the skillet from the heat.

Remove the cooked chicken from the skillet, cool slightly, and separate the meat from the bones. Return the meat to the pan. Add the rice, chicken stock, black pepper, oregano, and salt. Cover and simmer for 15 to 20 minutes, until the mixture has absorbed most of the water. (It should still be a little soupy.) Stir in the peas, black beans, grated Parmesan, and capers and cook for another 2 minutes over low heat. Serve immediately.

Yield: 3 to 4 servings

Nasi Goreng

Indonesia

This is the most common Indonesian dish—fried rice, eaten at any time of day on the islands. Nasi goreng is also the centerpiece of *rijstafel*, (means "rice table" in Dutch), a traditional buffet of an assortment of soups, meats, fish and vegetables served at the table at once. Nasi goreng is a perfect one-dish meal that can be refrigerated and reheated later in the microwave.

Ketjap manis, a sweetened soy sauce, is available at Asian food stores.

1 cup uncooked long-grain rice
2 cups water or chicken stock
3 tablespoons peanut or vegetable oil
1/2 pound skinless, boneless chicken thighs or
   pork loin, diced, or peeled and deveined shrimp
1 small onion, minced
4 shallots, minced
1 to 2 chile peppers, seeded and minced
1 tablespoon ketjap manis (If unavailable,
   combine 1 teaspoon brown sugar with 1
   tablespoon soy sauce)
1/2 teaspoon ground cumin
1/2 teaspoon ground coriander

Place the rice and water in a saucepan and cook over medium heat, covered, for 15 to 20 minutes, until the rice absorbs all the water. Fluff the rice and let it cool, then refrigerate for 2 hours.

Heat the oil in a skillet and add the chicken (or pork or shrimp). Saute for 5 to 7 minutes, until the chicken is done in the center. Remove the chicken from the skillet and add the onion, shallots, and chile peppers. Saute for about 3 minutes, until the vegetables are soft. Stir in the ketjap manis, cumin and coriander. Add the rice and stir continuously until it is browned. Return the chicken and continue to stir until the mixture is thoroughly heated. Serve immediately.

Yield: 4 servings

Duck with Passion Fruit-Fig Sauce

Hawaii

While driving along the north shore of Oahu, I visited a roadside fruit stand. Sharing space with the mangoes and apple bananas were some intriguing orange and yellow fruits about the size of a golf ball. The vendor sliced one open for me to try. Inside was a mesh of tiny edible seeds. I slurped the seedy pulp out of the shell, and my mouth savored the tropical flavors of pineapple, citrus, and guava. It was the refreshing and tongue-tingling pulp of the passion fruit.

Although passion fruit is more commonly used in fruit juices and desserts, their citrusy flavor is a natural complement to duck and chicken, which benefits from mildly acidic sauces. When buying passion fruit, look for mature specimens that are wrinkly, dimpled like a golf ball, firm, and slightly heavy. The figs add an earthy sweetness to this sauce. Passion fruits are a Frieda's Finest product, available in specialty food stores—and occasionally available fresh at large supermarkets.

1 duck, about 5 pounds, washed and patted dry

Sauce
1/2 cup dried and pitted figs, dates, or apricots, diced
1/4 cup red wine vinegar
1/4 cup diced red onion
1 tablespoon brown sugar
1/4 teaspoon white pepper
1/4 teaspoon freshly ground black pepper
Pulp of 8 passion fruits, strained (about 1/2 cup)

Preheat the oven to 400 degrees F.

Place the duck on a rack in a roasting pan and roast for 30 minutes. Reduce the heat to 350 degrees F and roast for an additional 45 minutes, basting every 15 minutes with the pan juices.

To make the sauce, place the figs, onion, vinegar, brown sugar and seasonings in a saucepan and cook for 3 to 4 minutes. Add the strained passion fruit pulp and simmer for 2 to 3 minutes more, stirring occasionally. Transfer the mixture to a food processor fitted with a steel blade and process for 15 seconds. Pour the sauce into a serving bowl.

To serve, remove the duck from the roasting pan with slotted spoons and cut it into quarters, removing the backbone. Spoon the sauce over the duck and pass the extra at the table.

Yield: 3 to 4 servings

Chicken and Pork Jambalaya

West Indies

Jambalaya (pronounced *jum-buh-LIE-ya*) is a hearty rice dish made with any combination of beef, poultry, pork, or seafood. All of the ingredients are tossed together with Creole Sauce, and the result is similar to Spanish paella, only much spicier. Some of the jambalaya dishes I have served at my restaurant are shrimp and ham; chicken, chorizo, and scallops; and vegetables and black beans.

3 tablespoons butter
1 pound skinless, boneless chicken breasts, diced
1 pound pork loin, trimmed and diced
4 cups Creole Sauce (page 110)
5 cups cooked white rice

Melt the butter in a large skillet and add the chicken and pork. Saute over moderate heat, stirring occasionally.

When the chicken and pork are white in the center, reduce the heat to medium, add the Creole Sauce, and bring to a simmer. Simmer for 30 seconds, stirring frequently. Add the rice to the skillet and blend all of the ingredients together. Continue cooking for 2 to 3 minutes, until the mixture is steaming.

Ladle the jambalaya onto 4 warm plates and serve with warm bread.

Yield: 4 servings

Bangkok Beef Curry

Thailand

Thai curries radiate a potent mixture of warm, sharp, and earthy flavors. Curry paste and chile peppers are balanced by the smooth blend of coconut milk, fish sauce, and lime leaves. Laos, or galanga, adds a mild, gingerlike nuance to the curry. Laos, in fact, looks like a prehistoric ginger root. It is available dried in Asian grocery stores and the specialty sections of large supermarkets.

1 1/2 cups coconut milk, fresh or canned, unsweetened
1 to 2 tablespoons red curry paste
1 1/2 pounds top round beef or sirloin tips, cubed
4 to 6 Kaffir lime leaves
1 Thai pepper, seeded and minced
2 tablespoons fish sauce or soy sauce
1 teaspoon laos (ground galanga, available where Asian foods are sold) or minced fresh ginger
1/2 cup fresh basil
4 cups cooked jasmine rice

Heat the coconut milk and curry paste in a wok or large skillet, stirring frequently. When the mixture begins to simmer, add the beef, lime leaves, chile pepper, fish sauce, and laos. Cook over medium heat for 8 to 10 minutes, stirring occasionally. Add the basil and cook for 1 minute more. Remove the lime leaves and pour the mixture over the cooked rice. Serve immediately.

Yield: 4 servings

Calypso Steak

West Indies

Barbecuing steaks is more of an American pastime than a Caribbean one, but the West Indian inclination for spirited food inspired this rum-and-lime-soaked steak.

Marinade

1/2 cup rum
1/4 cup lime juice
1/4 cup worcestershire sauce
1/4 cup vegetable oil
2 cloves garlic, minced
1 tablespoon minced fresh parsley
2 teaspoons minced fresh ginger
1 teaspoon ground allspice
1 teaspoon ground cloves
1 teaspoon red pepper flakes

4 strip streaks, 8 ounces each, well trimmed

Combine all of the marinade ingredients in a shallow baking dish. Add the steaks and marinate in the refrigerator for 4 to 6 hours. Turn the steaks after 3 hours.

Preheat the grill until the coals are gray to white.

Remove the steaks from the marinade and place on the lightly oiled grill. Cook for 4 to 5 minutes, then turn. Continue grilling until the steaks reach the desired degree of doneness.

Serve immediately with Thyme Mustard Sauce or Papaya Mustard Sauce.

Yield: 4 servings

Ropa Vieja

Puerto Rico

Ropa vieja means old clothes or old rope in Spanish. Traditionally, this was prepared with leftover or other tough cuts of meat shredded and stewed in a sauce of tomatoes, onions, bell peppers, and garlic. Although I have stayed true to the authentic recipe, I usually add a few drops of Scotch Bonnet Nectar at the table. For a hearty, economical meal, serve ropa vieja over rice.

2 tablespoons vegetable oil
1 large onion, diced
1 large bell pepper, seeded and diced
1 fresh tomato, diced
2 cloves garlic, minced
1 1/2 pounds cooked flank steak, shredded
1 can (9 ounces) whole tomatoes
1 tablespoon capers, drained
1/2 teaspoon freshly ground black pepper
1/4 teaspoon salt

In a large skillet, heat the oil and add the onion, bell pepper, fresh tomato, and garlic. Saute for about 5 minutes. Add the shredded steak, canned tomatoes, capers, and seasonings and simmer for about 10 minutes, stirring occasionally. Serve immediately over rice.

Yield: 4 servings

SCOTCH BONNET NECTAR

10 to 12 Scotch bonnet peppers, seeded and minced
1/2 cup peeled, diced carrots
1/2 cup diced fresh mango, peach, nectarine, or papaya
3 tablespoons minced shallots
1 cup red wine vinegar
1/4 cup lime juice
2 cloves garlic, minced
2 tablespoons brown sugar

Place all of the ingredients in a nonreactive saucepan and cook over medium heat. Simmer for 15 minutes, stirring occasionally and lowering the heat as the mixture begins to thicken.

Remove from the heat and allow the sauce to cool to room temperature. Transfer to a food processor fitted with a steel blade and process for 15 to 20 seconds, until the mixture is smooth. If refrigerated, the condiment should keep for several weeks.

Yield: 1 1/2 cups

Lemongrass-Grilled Beef

Vietnam

Lemongrass has been called the cilantro of the nineties (as cilantro was the ginger of the eighties and ginger was the garlic of the seventies). The fibrous herb imparts a subtle, lemony flavor to a variety of soups, marinades, and sauces. When using lemongrass, peel off and discard the outer green layer. Use the lower, pale-green half of the stalk, and mince as you do with ginger or garlic. Vietnamese-style of cooking often relies on the presence of this aromatic herb. Here it combines with fish sauce and lime juice to form a tangy marinade for beef.

1/3 cup fish sauce or soy sauce
2 1/2 tablespoons lime juice
2 1/2 tablespoons minced fresh lemongrass
1 tablespoon peanut or vegetable oil
2 cloves garlic, minced
1 chile pepper, seeded and minced
1/4 cup fresh mint leaves
1 tablespoon brown sugar
1 1/2 pounds top sirloin, sliced thinly into 2-inch strips
1 teaspoon sesame seeds

Combine the fish sauce, lime juice, lemongrass, oil, garlic, chile pepper, mint leaves, and brown sugar in a food processor fitted with a steel blade. Process for 15 to 20 seconds, forming a paste. Transfer the lemongrass paste to a shallow baking dish.

Thread the beef onto skewers. Add the beef to the marinade and cover completely. Refrigerate for 2 to 4 hours, or overnight, turning at least once.

When ready to prepare, preheat the grill until the coals are gray to white.

Place the skewered beef onto the lightly oiled grill. Grill each side for 2 to 3 minutes or to desired doneness. Transfer to warm plates and sprinkle with sesame seeds. Serve with Pineapple Fried Rice or over a salad of fresh greens with your favorite dressing.

Yield: 4 servings

Cheeseburger in Paradise

Hawaii

In Haleiwa, in northern Oahu, far from tourist-filled Honolulu, is the home of the world's best hamburger. Anyway, that's what the sign says at the Kua'aina restaurant. Actually, the hamburger was quite good. Burgers and fries, although not the paragon of island cuisine, can be good beach food once in a while. Here, then, is my homage to the Kua'aina sandwich, with a spicy twist.

Chile Pepper Catsup

3 tomatoes, diced
1/2 cup diced onion
2 to 3 chile peppers, seeded and minced
2 cloves garlic, minced
1/2 cup red wine vinegar
1/2 cup canned crushed tomato
1/4 cup water
1/4 cup brown sugar
1/2 teaspoon chili powder
2 to 3 teaspoons red hot sauce
1/2 teaspoon freshly ground black pepper
1/4 teaspoon salt

Burgers

1 1/2 pounds lean ground beef
1 bell pepper, seeded and minced
1 medium-size onion, minced
2 jalapeño peppers, seeded and minced
1 tablespoon red hot sauce
2 teaspoons dried thyme
1 teaspoon red pepper flakes
4 slices provolone or Monterey jack cheese,
    1 ounce each
4 hamburger rolls, warmed
1 large tomato, sliced
4 to 5 leaves romaine or leaf lettuce, washed and
    torn

To make the catsup, combine the tomatoes, onion, chile peppers, garlic, vinegar, crushed tomatoes, water, brown sugar, and seasonings and bring to a simmer over medium heat. Simmer for 20 to 25 minutes, stirring occasionally. Remove from the heat and puree mixture in a food processor fitted with a steel blade (or in a blender) for 30 seconds. The catsup will still be slightly chunky. Set aside.

To make the burgers, combine the ground beef, bell pepper, onion, and jalapeño peppers in a large bowl. Mix in the red hot sauce and seasonings and shape the meat into 4 patties.

Grill or pan-fry the burgers until they are cooked to the desired doneness. Melt 1 slice of cheese on each burger a few seconds before placing them on the warmed buns. Spoon the catsup onto each burger and top with tomato and lettuce.

Yield: 4 servings

Jamaican Beef Patties

Jamaica

Although many of the Caribbean islands boast their own versions of patties, or pastries stuffed with meat, the Jamaican beef patty is the most famous. It is a descendant of the Spanish turnover, the empanada. The most common filling is ground beef seasoned with turmeric, onions, hot peppers, and thyme, spooned into a flaky dough and baked. I serve this patty with a variety of condiments, such as Chile Pepper Catsup, Tomatillo Hot Sauce, Sofrito, or Papaya Mustard Sauce.

Pastry

2 cups all-purpose flour
1/2 teaspoon baking powder
1/2 teaspoon salt
1/2 cup margarine or shortening
1/4 cup water

Meat Filling

1 pound finely ground beef
1 medium-size onion, minced
1 Scotch bonnet or jalapeño pepper, seeded and
   minced
1/4 cup water or chicken stock
3 tablespoons bread crumbs
1/2 teaspoon turmeric
1/2 teaspoon curry powder
1/2 teaspoon freshly ground black pepper
1/4 teaspoon salt
1 egg, beaten

To make the pastry, combine the flour, baking powder, and salt in a mixing bowl. With a pastry cutter or a knife and fork, cut in the margarine until the mixture resembles coarse meal. Mix in the water gradually to form a ball. Refrigerate the dough for 15 minutes.

For the filling, saute the beef, onion, Scotch bonnet pepper, water, bread crumbs, turmeric, curry powder, black pepper, and salt in a large skillet. Cook for 7 to 10 minutes, until the beef is lightly browned.

Divide the dough into 4 equal-sized balls. With a rolling pin, roll each ball into a thin circle. Spoon the beef mixture into one-half of each circle and fold the dough over, enclosing the beef. Seal the edges with a fork. With a pastry brush, lightly brush the egg wash over the top of each patty.

Place the patties on a lightly greased baking sheet. Bake the patties for 20 minutes, until the dough is light brown. Serve immediately.

Yield: 4 servings

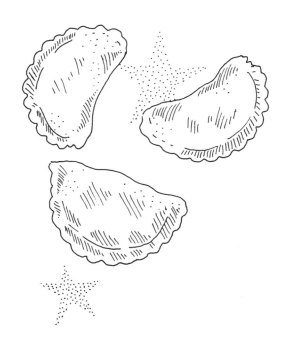

Pork Sancocho

Dominican Republic

Sancocho refers to stewed meat, fish, or vegetables, and it is prepared in a variety of ways throughout the Caribbean. The version served in the Dominican Republic is packed with plantains, cassava, potatoes, okra, and whatever else is in the kitchen. This is a super stew.

1/4 pound salt pork, diced
1 1/2 pounds boneless pork loin, cubed
1 medium-size onion, diced
1 medium-size bell pepper, seeded and diced
1 Scotch bonnet pepper, seeded and minced
1 tablespoon minced fresh parsley
1 medium-size sweet potato, scrubbed and diced
1 green plantain, peeled and diced
1/2 pound cassava or yuca, peeled and diced
1 cup cooked okra, sliced
4 cups water or chicken stock
1 teaspoon freshly ground black pepper
1/2 teaspoon salt

Cook the salt pork in a large saucepan for 5 to 7 minutes over medium heat, stirring frequently. Remove the salt pork and discard, leaving the rendered fat in the pan. Add the pork loin to the pan and saute for 7 minutes, until the pork is brown. Transfer the pork to a warm plate.

Add the onion, bell pepper, Scotch bonnet pepper, and parsley to the saucepan and saute for 5 minutes. Remove the pork to the pan, then add the sweet potato, plantain, cassava, okra, water, black pepper, and salt. Bring the mixture to a simmer over medium heat and cook uncovered for 45 minutes to 1 hour, stirring occasionally.

Remove the stew from the heat and serve immediately.

Yield: 4 servings

Pork and Chicken Adobo

Philippines

Adobo, the national dish of the Philipines, is essentially a stew of meat or fish in soy, vinegar, and garlic. It has a pickled, almost sour flavor—ideal for serving over bland rice or noodles that need spicing up.

3/4 pound pork loin, diced
3/4 pound boneless chicken thighs
1 onion, diced
2 cloves garlic, minced
1 tablespoon minced fresh ginger
1/2 cup soy sauce
1/2 cup red wine or rice vinegar
3 bay leaves
1 teaspoon freshly ground black pepper
3 cups water

Combine all of the ingredients, except the water, and marinate for 3 to 4 hours.

Transfer the mixture to a saucepan and add the water. Bring the mixture to a boil and simmer for about 1 hour.

Remove the pork and chicken and bay leaves from the liquid. Discard the bay leaves and arrange the meat on serving plates. Reduce the remaining liquid over high heat, stirring frequently. Pour the sauce over the meat. Serve immediately.

Yield: 3 to 4 servings

Thai Pork Curry with Basil

Thailand

Thai curries are prepared from a spicy paste of herbs, roots, leaves, and chile peppers. Several types of curry pastes are available: red, green, yellow, masamun, panang, and others. The addition of coconut milk during the cooking tempers the heat and produces a rich, piquant sauce. The curry paste can be made or purchased at Asian groceries. (Thai curries are different from Caribbean and Indian curries, which are prepared from dry seasonings and without coconut.)

1 teaspoon cornstarch
1 teaspoon water
2 tablespoons peanut or vegetable oil
1 1/2 pounds boneless pork loin, diced
1 cup diced, unpeeled eggplant
2 cloves garlic, minced
1 Thai pepper or jalapeño pepper, seeded and minced
1 1/2 teaspoons green or red curry paste
1 cup coconut milk, fresh or canned, unsweetened
1/4 cup soy sauce
2 teaspoons oyster sauce
1/2 cup fresh basil leaves, chopped

In a small bowl, combine the corn starch and water. Set aside.

Heat the oil in a skillet or wok. Add the pork and eggplant and saute for 5 to 7 minutes, until the pork is almost completely done in the center. Add the garlic, Thai pepper, and curry paste and saute for 2 to 3 minutes more, until the pork is completely cooked.

Add the coconut milk, soy sauce, oyster sauce and the cornstarch mixture. Bring to a simmer, stirring frequently. Add the basil leaves and cook for another 2 minutes. Serve immediately over rice.

Yield: 2 to 3 servings

Grilled Pork with Apricot Catsup

Hawaii

Fresh apricots resemble a little globe of sunshine. Although they usually are only available in early summer, they are well worth the wait. I enjoy incorporating apricots into a variety of condiments, such as mustards, chutneys, and catsups. In Hawaii, apricots frequently are paired with roast or marinated pork. Apricot catsup makes a fruity companion to this lightly marinated pork loin.

Marinade

1/2 cup soy sauce
1/3 cup pineapple juice
1/4 cup red wine vinegar
2 cloves garlic, minced
2 tablespoons minced fresh ginger
2 tablespoons honey
1/2 teaspoon freshly ground black pepper

1 1/2 pounds pork loin, well trimmed

Catsup

4 apricots, pitted and chopped
1 cup red wine vinegar
1/2 cup red onion, diced
1/4 cup brown sugar
1 1/2 tablespoons minced fresh ginger
1 clove garlic, minced
1/4 teaspoon freshly ground black pepper
1/4 teaspoon salt

To prepare the marinade, combine the soy sauce, pineapple juice, vinegar, garlic, ginger, honey, and pepper in a mixing bowl. Add the pork loin and marinate for 3 to 4 hours.

To prepare the catsup, combine the apricots, vinegar, onion, sugar, ginger, garlic, pepper and salt in a saucepan. Cook for 10 to 12 minutes over medium heat, stirring occasionally. Remove the mixture from the heat and transfer to a food processor fitted with a steel blade. Process for 20 to 30 seconds, until the mixture is smooth. Pour into a serving bowl.

Preheat the grill until the coals are gray to white.

Remove the pork from the marinade and drain. Discard the marinade. Place the pork on the lightly oiled grill and cook for 5 to 7 minutes on each side, until the pork is done in the center. Transfer to warm plates and spoon the apricot catsup over the pork. Pass the extra catsup at the table.

Yield: 4 servings

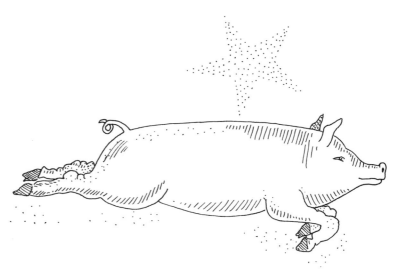

Pineapple-Barbecued Ribs

Hawaii

Maybe it's because of their size, but I grew up thinking pineapples grew on large trees, probably something the size of a palm tree. Wrong. Pineapples grow on plants about 2 feet high. It is a most majestic-looking plant, however. I also found out, after visiting pineapple plantations in Hawaii, that pineapple juice comes from the cores of processed pineapples.

Here is a Hawaiian twist to the traditional barbecued rib recipe. Adding pineapple and soy to the marinade recipe produces a fruity and scrumptious result. Have lots of napkins handy for this one.

1 medium-size onion, diced
1 large tomato, diced
1 cup diced fresh pineapple
3 to 4 cloves garlic, minced
2 chile peppers, seeded and minced
2 tablespoons minced fresh ginger
2 tablespoons Dijon-style mustard
3/4 cup red wine vinegar
1/2 cup pineapple juice
1/2 cup soy sauce
1/4 cup worcestershire sauce
1/4 cup canned crushed tomatoes
1/4 cup molasses
1/4 cup brown sugar
1 teaspoon freshly ground black pepper
3 to 6 pounds spare ribs

To prepare the barbecue sauce, place all of the ingredients, except the ribs, in a large saucepan. Simmer over medium heat for 15 to 20 minutes, stirring occasionally. Allow to cool, then transfer to a food processor fitted with a steel blade. Process for 15 to 20 seconds. Pour into a bowl.

When you are ready to prepare the ribs, preheat the oven to 375 degrees F. Arrange the ribs in a single layer on a baking sheet. Roast for 1 to 1 1/2 hours, until the meat pulls easily from the bone.

While the ribs are in the oven, preheat the grill until the coals are gray to white. Finish cooking the ribs on a lightly greased grill, basting with the barbecue sauce. Grill until the ribs reach the desired tenderness, turning and basting frequently. Pass the extra sauce at the table. Serve with Green Papaya Salad.

Yield: 4 to 6 servings

Curried Lamb Pie

Trinidad

2 tablespoons butter
1 medium-size onion, diced
3 cloves garlic, minced
2 tomatoes, diced
1 chile pepper, seeded and minced
Juice of 1 lime
2 tablespoons curry powder
1 teaspoon fresh thyme leaves
1/2 teaspoon ground coriander
1/2 teaspoon ground allspice
1/4 teaspoon ground turmeric
1 pound cubed lamb, well trimmed
1 cup diced, unpeeled, scrubbed potatoes
1/2 cup water
1/4 cup fresh mint leaves, minced
1 pound puff pastry dough or Stuffed Roti Dough
   (page 86)

Preheat the oven to 400 degrees F.

Place the butter, onion, and garlic in a skillet and saute for 2 minutes. Add the tomatoes, chile pepper, and seasonings and saute for another 2 minutes. Stir in the lamb, potatoes, and lime juice and cook for 10 minutes more. Add the water and cook for another 5 minutes, stirring occasionally. Stir in the mint leaves.

Roll out the pastry dough into two 10-inch circles. Arrange one layer in the bottom of a 9-inch round cake pan. Cover the dough with the lamb mixture. Cover the filling with the remaining circle of dough. Pinch the edges together to seal. Bake for 12 to 15 minutes, until the crust is lightly brown. Serve immediately.

Yield: 6 to 8 servings

Tamarind Lamb Satay

Indonesia

Lamb satays are frequently marinated in a peanut butter/tamarind mixture, with a hint of ginger, garlic, and mint. Serve this satay with Lime-Peanut Dipping Sauce, Indonesian Peanut Sauce, or over a salad of fresh greens, in the spirit of Thai Grilled Beef Salad.

4 ounces dried tamarind (available where Asian
   foods are sold)
1 cup water
1/2 cup peanut butter
1/4 cup soy sauce
3 cloves garlic, minced
1/4 cup fresh mint leaves
2 tablespoons peanut or vegetable oil
2 tablespoons lime juice
1 tablespoon minced fresh ginger
1 chile pepper, seeded and minced
2 teaspoons ground coriander
2 teaspoons ground cumin
1/2 teaspoon freshly ground black pepper
1 1/2 pounds lamb cubes, well trimmed

Combine the water and dried tamarind and set aside for 30 minutes, stirring occasionally. Drain the mixture through a sieve. Save the liquid and discard the pulp.

Add the tamarind liquid, peanut butter, soy sauce, garlic, mint leaves, oil, lime juice, ginger, chile pepper, coriander, cumin, and black pepper to a food processor fitted with a steel blade. Process for 15 to 20 seconds, forming a paste. Set aside. Thread the lamb cubes onto 10-inch-long metal or bamboo skewers and place in a rectangular casserole dish. Pour the tamarind marinade over the skewers and refrigerate for 2 to 4 hours. Turn the skewers after 1 hour.

Preheat the grill until the coals are gray to white.

Place the skewered lamb on a lightly oiled grill. Turn after 4 to 5 minutes. Grill each side until the meat reaches the desired degree of doneness. Transfer to warm plates and serve immediately.

Yield: 4 servings

Stuffed Roti

Trinidad

Roti is a fat sandwich filled with curried vegetables, seafood, or chicken. Rotis originated in Trinidad, where the Indians came to work in the sugar plantations and wrapped their traditional flat bread around their curries for lunch, or whenever they were given a chance to eat. Trinidad has since become both a roti and a curry capital. Rotis are often served from roadside stands throughout the West Indies—the Caribbean version of fast food. Potatoes, chickpeas, and pumpkin are some of my favorite filling ingredients.

4 cups all-purpose flour
2 teaspoons baking powder
1 teaspoon salt
1/4 cup oil
1 cup water (to mix)
1 tablespoon butter, melted
3 to 4 cups Sweet Potato and Chickpea Filling or
    Chicken and Pumpkin Filling (see below)

Combine the dry ingredients in a mixing bowl. Gradually add the oil and water while mixing and kneading the dough. Set the dough aside for about 15 minutes.

Divide the dough into 4 to 6 equal-sized balls. Flatten each slightly and roll out into 8 inch squares. Fill the middle of each square with about 1/2 cup of the filling. Wrap the dough around the mixture to seal the filling inside.

To cook the roti, place the butter in a skillet over high heat until it sizzles. Reduce the heat to medium and place the rotis in the pan. Cook for 2 to 3 minutes, until the crust is light brown. Turn with a wide spatula and continue cooking. Repeat the process with the remaining rotis. Serve immediately.

Yield: 4 large servings

Sweet Potato and Chickpea Filling

2 tablespoons butter, melted
2 to 3 cloves garlic, minced
1 small red onion, diced
1 large sweet potato, scrubbed and diced
1 1/4 cups water
1 1/2 tablespoons curry powder
1 teaspoon red hot sauce
1/8 teaspoon salt
1 can (16 ounce) chickpeas, drained

To make the filling, place the butter, garlic, and onion in a deep skillet and saute for 3 to 4 minutes over medium heat. Add the potato, water, curry powder, red hot sauce, and salt and cook for about 15 minutes, until the potatoes are soft but not mushy. Add the chickpeas and cook for another 5 to 10 minutes, stirring occasionally. Set the filling aside.

Chicken and Pumpkin Filling

2 tablespoons butter, melted
3 to 4 cloves garlic, minced
1/2 cup diced red onion
1 Scotch bonnet or jalapeño pepper, seeded and minced
2 tablespoons curry powder
1 to 2 teaspoons red hot sauce
1 teaspoon ground coriander
1/2 teaspoon salt
4 cups diced fresh pumpkin
2 cups water
1 pound cooked, boneless chicken, diced

To make the filling, place the butter, garlic, onion, and Scotch bonnet pepper in a saucepan and saute for 3 to 4 minutes. Add the curry powder, red hot sauce, coriander, and salt and saute for another 2 minutes. Add the pumpkin and water and cook over medium heat for 20 minutes, stirring occasionally. Stir in the chicken and simmer for another 2 to 3 minutes. Set aside.

Salads,
Vegetables,
&
Side Dishes

Aloha Chicken Salad

Hawaii

Here is a tangy salad ideal for a light lunch on a hot sunny day. The sweet and tart flavor of pineapple inspired this light, herbal dressing for chicken. For a special touch, serve the salad in the hollowed-out pineapple shell.

Vinaigrette

1 cup chopped fresh pineapple
1/2 cup white wine vinegar
1 tablespoon honey
1/2 tablespoon minced fresh cilantro
1 teaspoon fresh thyme leaves
1/2 teaspoon white pepper
1/4 teaspoon ground allspice
1/4 teaspoon salt
1/4 cup vegetable or olive oil

Salad

1 pound poached chicken meat, diced
1 mango, peeled, pitted, and diced
1 cup diced fresh pineapple
3/4 cup minced celery

To make the vinaigrette, place the chopped pineapple and the vinegar in a nonreactive saucepan. Cook for 5 minutes over medium heat. Transfer to a bowl and cool the mixture in the refrigerator for about 30 minutes.

Add the cooled pineapple mixture, plus the honey, cilantro, thyme, white pepper, allspice, and salt to a food processor fitted with a steel blade. Blend for 20 to 30 seconds or until the mixture is smooth. Slowly drizzle in the oil while the motor is running, and process for 15 to 20 seconds more.

In a mixing bowl, combine the vinaigrette with the chicken, mango, pineapple, and celery in a mixing bowl. Refrigerate for at least 1 hour. Serve on a bed of leaf lettuce.

Yield: 4 servings

Lime Chicken and Pasta Salad

Thailand

Limes are prevalent ingredients in many Thai meals. There are two kinds: the bumpy, dark green Kaffir limes (prized for their leaves and rind) and the small, dark-green Thai limes (valued for their sweet juice). The flavor of lime often is juxtaposed with salty fish sauces and pungent curry sauces.

1/2 cup fish or soy sauce
1/4 cup lime juice
2 tablespoons vegetable oil
1 tablespoon sesame oil
1 tablespoon minced fresh lemongrass
1 tablespoon lime zest
2 teaspoons minced fresh ginger
1 clove garlic, minced
1 Thai pepper or jalapeño pepper, seeded and minced
1/2 pound pasta spirals, cooked
1 pound chicken breasts, cooked and diced
6 to 8 broccoli florets, blanched
1 red bell pepper, seeded and slivered
1/2 cup slivered water chestnuts, fresh or canned

In a large mixing bowl, combine the soy sauce, lime juice, vegetable oil, sesame oil, lemongrass, lime zest, ginger, garlic, and chile pepper. Add the pasta, chicken, broccoli, bell pepper, and water chestnuts and toss well. Refrigerate for at least 1 hour and toss again before serving.

Yield: 3 to 4 servings

Yam Yai

Thailand

In Thai cuisine, the salad often is a one-dish meal. Yam Yai—Big Thai Salad, as we call it at my restaurant—encompasses many of the flavors of Thailand and the islands of Southeast Asia. Chicken, pork, and shellfish are tossed with noodles and a variety of crunchy vegetables and herbs. The salads, or yams, often are flavored with fish sauce, lime juice, and chile peppers. If fish sauce is too strong for your palate, light soy sauce is an acceptable substitute.

4 ounces uncooked cellophane noodles
1/2 pound boneless, cooked chicken meat, diced
20 to 24 cooked medium-size shrimp, peeled and deveined
4 green onions, minced
4 radishes, slivered
1 cup shredded bok choy, kale, or spinach
1 cup bean sprouts
1 clove garlic, minced
1 Thai pepper or jalapeño pepper, seeded and minced
1/4 cup fish or soy sauce
2 tablespoons lime juice
2 tablespoons vegetable oil
2 tablespoons fresh basil leaves
1 teaspoon brown sugar

Place the cellophane noodles in hot water for 5 to 7 minutes, remove from heat, and then drain.

Combine all of the remaining ingredients in a large mixing bowl. Add the drained noodles and toss thoroughly. Refrigerate 1 hour before serving. Arrange on a bed of leafy green lettuce.

Yield: 4 servings

Javanese Fried Noodles

Indonesia

Indonesia is a sprawling nation composed of thousands of island—including Bali, Sumatra, Borneo, and Java—filled with beaches, volcanoes, rice paddies, and strong coffee. Of these islands, Java is the largest and most populous. Fried noodles are a staple of Javanese restaurants.

8 ounces uncooked rice noodles
3 tablespoons peanut or vegetable oil
1/2 pound diced chicken thighs or breast
2 cloves garlic, minced
1 chile pepper, seeded and minced
1 1/2 tablespoons minced shallots
2 tomatoes, diced
2 Thai or 1 small regular eggplant, diced (about 1 cup)
1 cup shredded kale or bok choy
2 ounces bean sprouts
1 tablespoon ketjap manis, fish sauce, or soy sauce
1 teaspoon sugar
1 tablespoon minced fresh cilantro

Place the noodles in hot water to cover for 5 minutes. Remove from the heat and drain the noodles in a colander. Cool under running water.

In a large skillet or wok, heat the oil until it sizzles. Add the chicken and saute for 5 to 7 minutes, until the meat is done in the center.

Remove the chicken from the skillet and add the garlic, chile pepper, shallots, tomatoes, and eggplants. Saute for 3 to 4 minutes. Add the kale, bean sprouts, ketjap manis, and sugar and saute for 2 to 3 minutes more. Stir in the chicken and noodles and cook for about 3 minutes, until the noodles and chicken are heated through. Serve immediately.

Yield: 4 servings

Pineapple Fried Rice

Thailand

Jasmine rice is a sweet, delicate rice prevalent in Thai cuisine. Leftover rice often is fried the next day for lunch. It also is common for Thai fried rice to include pineapple, which lends a sweet-and-sour, fruity flavor to the meal. Add a dash of elegance by serving the fried rice in a hollowed-out pineapple shell.

1 cup jasmine or long grain rice
2 cups water
3 tablespoons peanut or vegetable oil
1/2 pound uncooked chicken breast or pork loin, diced
12 to 16 large shrimp, peeled, deveined and butterflied
1 medium-size onion, diced
1 cup diced fresh pineapple
2 cloves garlic, minced
1 Thai pepper or jalapeno pepper, seeded and minced
2 tablespoons fish sauce or soy sauce
1 cup shredded bok choy

Place the rice and water in a saucepan and cook over medium heat, covered, for 15 to 20 minutes, until the rice absorbs all the water. Fluff the rice and let it cool, then transfer to a bowl and refrigerate for 2 hours.

Heat the oil in a skillet and add the shrimp and the pork or chicken. Saute for 5 to 7 minutes, until the shrimp are pink and the pork or chicken is done in the center. Remove the shrimp and meat from the skillet and set aside. To the skillet, add the onion, pineapple, garlic, and chile pepper. Saute for about 3 minutes, until the vegetables are soft. Stir in the fish sauce and bok choy. Add the chilled rice and stir the mixture continuously until it is lightly browned. Return the shrimp and meat to the skillet and continue to stir until the mixture is heated through. Serve immediately.

Yield: 4 servings

Citrus Duck Salad

Pacific Rim

I never ate duck while growing up—it was the province of expensive haughty restaurants, and always served with a boring orange sauce. Many Southeast Asians, Thai, and Indonesians are avid duck eaters, and prepare duck in a variety of ways. Here is a refreshing duck salad with citrus and Asian flavors.

1 duck, about 5 pounds, washed and patted dry
4 ounces cellophane noodles
4 green onions, minced
4 radishes, slivered
2 cloves garlic, minced
1 chile pepper, seeded and minced
2 seedless oranges, peeled and sectioned
1 cup bean sprouts
1/2 cup orange juice
1/4 cup soy sauce
1/4 cup tamarind liquid or lime juice
1 tablespoon sesame oil

Preheat the oven to 400 degrees F.

Place the duck on a rack in a roasting pan and roast for 30 minutes. Reduce the heat to 350 degrees F. and bake for an additional 45 minutes, basting every 15 minutes with the pan juices.

Meanwhile, place the cellophane noodles in boiling water to cover, then remove from the heat and set aside for 10 minutes. Drain the noodles in a colander and cool them under running cold water. Place in a small bowl and refrigerate.

Remove the duck from the roasting pan and chill for 4 to 6 hours. Once chilled, remove the skin from the duck and debone the meat. Shred the meat and transfer it to a mixing bowl. Toss with the noodles and the remaining ingredients and refrigerate for at least 1 hour before serving.

Yield: 4 to 6 servings

Thai-Grilled Beef Salad

Thailand

This salad, along with Jamaican Jerk Chicken, is the all-time best-selling lunch item at my restaurant. Strips of beef are marinated in a Thai-inspired marinade, grilled over hot coals, and served on a bed of tossed greens with a variety of fresh vegetables. You'll say goodbye to boring chef's salad once you've eaten this.

Beef

1 1/2 cups soy sauce
1 cup worcestershire sauce
1 cup vegetable oil
2 tablespoons minced fresh ginger
6 to 8 cloves garlic, minced
2 to 3 chile peppers, seeded and minced
6 drops red hot sauce or hot oil
1 tablespoon dark sesame oil
1 tablespoon honey
1 teaspoon freshly ground black pepper
1/4 cup lime or orange juice
1 pound sirloin, trimmed and cut into 2-inch cubes

Salad

1 head leaf lettuce, washed and torn
1 cup Dijon-style mustard vinaigrette or your favorite salad dressing
1 tomato, cut into 8 wedges
2 bell peppers, seeded and cut into strips
2 small red onions, cut into 1/4-inch slices
1 avocado, peeled, pitted, and quartered
1 large carrot, peeled and shredded
2 ounces alfalfa or bean sprouts

To prepare the marinade, whisk together all the marinade ingredients. Place the beef cubes in the marinade and refrigerate for at least 4 hours, rearranging and tossing the cubes after about 2 hours.

Preheat the grill until the coals are gray to white. Meanwhile, mound the leaf lettuce on 4 dinner plates and drizzle the vinaigrette over the greens. Arrange the tomato, bell peppers, onions, avocado, carrot, and sprouts around the circumference.

When you are ready to grill the meat, drain the marinated cubes in a colander. (It is important to drain the meat first, as grilling the cubes straight from the marinade will cause excessive flare-up.) Discard the marinade.

Place the cubes in a row on the grill, and grill each side for 2 to 3 minutes or to desired doneness. Use tongs to turn the meat.

Arrange the grilled beef on the bed of greens on each plate. Serve immediately.

Yield: 4 servings

Note: The cubed meat may be threaded onto skewers before marinating.

Grilled Lobster-Medallion Salad

Pacific Rim

If I were in the kitchen alone with a lobster, I would have no trouble devouring the creature with reckless abandon: Boil, crack, and dip into butter. However, when I am in mixed company, and manners count, I feel stifled, wary, and a little goofy wearing a bib. Consequently, I have developed a recipe for polite people that involves lightly marinating lobster with the flavors of the Pacific Rim.

12 cups water
2 live lobsters, 2 pounds each
1/4 cup low sodium soy sauce
2 tablespoons peanut or vegetable oil
1 tablespoon minced fresh ginger
1 tablespoon minced fresh cilantro
1 tablespoon minced fresh lemongrass
1 chile pepper, seeded and minced
Juice of 1 lemon
1 tablespoon honey
1/2 teaspoon freshly ground black pepper
1 lemon, quartered

Bring the water to a boil and add the lobsters. Boil for 12 minutes, then drain. Cool the lobster slightly under cold running water. Remove the meat from the lobster tail and claws, picking out cartilage and bones. Slice the tail meat into 1-inch medallions.

Combine the soy sauce, oil, ginger, cilantro, lemongrass, chile pepper, lemon juice, honey, and black pepper in a mixing bowl. Place the lobster medallions and claw meat in the marinade and refrigerate for 1 to 2 hours.

Preheat the grill until the coals are gray to white.

Remove the lobster meat from the marinade with a slotted spoon and drain thoroughly. Arrange the meat on the lightly oiled grill and cook for 3 to 4 minutes. Turn the medallions and claw meat and continue cooking until the lobster is warmed through. Serve the lobster over a salad of fresh greens and vegetables (see Thai Grilled Beef Salad), or with Pumpkin Rice with Kale, Pineapple Fried Rice, or Gado-Gado. Squeeze the lemon wedges over the lobster before serving.

Yield: 3 to 4 servings

Polynesian Veggie Stir-Fry

Polynesia

Here is a healthy collection of vegetables tossed with soy sauce, chile-garlic paste, sesame oil, lime juice, and rice. Stir-fries are a Chinese influence in the cuisines of Thailand, Vietnam, and Indonesia.

8 broccoli florets
2 tablespoons peanut oil
4 tablespoons soy sauce
2 tablespoons lime juice
1 1/2 tablespoons minced fresh ginger
1 teaspoon sesame oil
1/4 teaspoon hot oil
1 to 2 teaspoons chile-garlic paste or red curry paste (available where Asian foods are sold)
12 ears canned baby corn
1 bell pepper, seeded and slivered
6 mushrooms, sliced
1 1/2 inches daikon (Japanese radish), thinly sliced
1/2 cup diced fresh pineapple
2 cups cooked rice
2 teaspoons minced fresh cilantro

Place the broccoli in boiling water to cover, cook for 3 minutes, and drain. Chill under cold running water and set aside.

To a wok, add the peanut oil, 2 tablespoons of the soy sauce, 1 tablespoon of the lime juice, ginger, sesame oil, hot oil, and chile paste. Heat until it sizzles, stirring frequently. Add the broccoli, baby corn, bell pepper, mushrooms, daikon, and pineapple, and cook for 5 to 7 minutes, stirring frequently.

Add the rice, the remaining 2 tablespoons of soy sauce, the remaining tablespoon lime juice, and the cilantro and toss thoroughly. Cook for 2 to 3 minutes longer, until the rice steams.

Remove the mixture to warm plates. Serve immediately with Papaya Mustard Sauce, Sambal, or Indonesian Peanut Sauce.

Yield: 4 side dish servings or 2 main dish servings

Pumpkin and Black-Eyed Pea Accras

West Indies

Accras (or akkras), also called fritters, are served throughout the Caribbean. Derived from the West African tradition of frying black-eyed-pea fritters, the fried batter now includes a variety of ingredients, such as fish, vegetables, and chile peppers. In Jamaica, Stamp-and-Go is a popular fritter of salted codfish and spices. Conch Fritters are a Bahamian invention.

Serve these pumpkin accras with Papaya Mustard Sauce, Creole Sauce, or Tamarind-Pepper Sauce.

4 cups diced calabaza or pumpkin, or 10 ounces canned mashed pumpkin
1 cup cooked black-eyed peas
1 egg, beaten
1/4 cup milk
2 cups all-purpose flour
1 chile pepper, seeded and minced
1/2 teaspoon freshly ground black pepper
1/4 teaspoon salt
Vegetable oil for frying

If using fresh pumpkin, place the pumpkin in boiling water to cover and cook for 12 minutes, until it is soft. Drain in a colander and cool under running cold water. (If using canned pumpkin, skip this step.)

Add the pumpkin and the black-eyed peas to a food processor fitted with a steel blade. Process for about 20 seconds, until the mixture is smooth. Transfer to a mixing bowl. Whisk in the egg and milk. Blend in the flour and seasonings.

Meanwhile, heat the vegetable oil to 375 degrees F. Gently drop about 1 tablespoon of dough into the oil. Repeat the process with the remaining dough. Fry for 10 to 12 minutes, until the accras are light and golden brown.

With a slotted spoon, remove the accras and place them on a paper towel. Serve as an appetizer with your favorite hot sauce or as a side dish with a spicy meal.

Yield: about 24 accras

Red Beans and Rice

West Indies

Beans and rice is prepared in a variety of ways throughout the Caribbean. Uncooked beans should be sorted for rocks and rinsed prior to cooking. Soaking the beans overnight (and changing and replenishing the water several times) will decrease the cooking time and yield a softer, plumper bean. Although many recipes call for chicken stock or ham hocks, I prefer a light vegetable stock or water. For an island spin, substitute 1/2 cup of coconut milk for 1/2 cup of water in the rice recipe.

Beans

2 1/2 cups vegetable stock or water
1 cup dried red, pink, or black beans, or pigeon
   peas, soaked overnight and drained
1/8 cup beer or dry red wine
1 chile pepper, seeded and minced (optional)
1 teaspoon ground cumin
1 teaspoon chili powder
1 teaspoon red hot sauce
1/2 teaspoon dried thyme
1/2 teaspoon freshly ground black pepper
1/2 teaspoon salt

Rice

2 cups vegetable stock or water
1 cup uncooked white rice
2 garlic cloves, minced
1 small onion, diced
1/2 teaspoon dried thyme
1/2 teaspoon ground cumin
1/2 teaspoon ground allspice
1/2 teaspoon black pepper
1/2 teaspoon salt

To prepare the beans, combine the vegetable stock, beans, beer, chile pepper, cumin, chili powder, red hot sauce, thyme, and black pepper in a sauce pan. Cook over low heat for about 1 hour, stirring occasionally. The beans should be soft, but not mushy. Stir in the salt and set aside.

To prepare the rice, combine the vegetable stock, rice, garlic, onion, thyme, cumin, allspice, black pepper, and salt in a sauce pan and cover. Cook over medium heat for 15 minutes, stirring occasionally. Stir in the cooked beans and continue cooking until the rice is fluffy, about 5 more minutes. Remove from the heat and serve immediately.

Yield: 4 servings

Gado-Gado

Indonesia

Gado-gado is a popular vegetarian dish found throughout Indonesia. It involves a variety of vegetables sauteed in a spicy peanut butter sauce and served with rice.

2 tablespoons peanut oil
1 medium-size onion, diced
1 bell pepper, seeded and diced
1 cup unpeeled, diced eggplant
6 mushrooms, sliced
1/2 cup shredded cabbage
6 to 8 broccoli florets, blanched
1 to 2 cloves garlic, minced
2 teaspoons minced fresh ginger
1 chile pepper, seeded and minced
1 cup bean sprouts
1 cup peanut butter
1/2 cup water
1/4 cup soy sauce or ketjap manis
2 tablespoons lime juice
1 tablespoon honey
1/2 teaspoon ground cumin
1/2 teaspoon ground coriander

In a large skillet, place the oil, onion, bell pepper, eggplant, mushrooms, and cabbage. Saute for 6 to 8 minutes over medium heat. Add the broccoli, garlic, ginger, chile pepper, and bean sprouts and continue to saute for 2 to 3 minutes more.

Stir in the peanut butter, water, soy sauce, lime juice, honey, and seasonings. Reduce the heat and cook for another 4 to 5 minutes, until the mixture is simmering. Stir the vegetables frequently. Serve immediately over rice.

Yield: 3 to 4 servings

MoBay Vegetables with Curried Coconut Sauce

Jamaica

Just outside "MoBay" (Montego Bay, Jamaica), on my way to the straw market, I discovered a small paradise of tropical vegetation. The gardener gave me a tour through the wonderland of plantains, bananas, breadfruits, callaloo, mangoes, papayas, calabazas, coconuts, eggplants, and my favorite peppers, Scotch bonnets.

This dish is an ode to that morning near MoBay. The flavors of curry and coconut create a delectable sauce for this cornucopia of tropical vegetables.

2 tablespoons butter
2 tablespoons all-purpose flour
4 cups diced fresh pumpkin
1 medium-size christophene or zucchini, diced
2 cups unpeeled, diced eggplant
1 cup peeled, diced breadfruit (optional)
2 cloves garlic, minced
1 Scotch bonnet pepper, seeded and minced
1 cup plus 1 tablespoon shredded fresh coconut
1 1/2 tablespoons curry powder
1/4 teaspoon salt
1/4 teaspoon ground allspice
1/8 teaspoon ground nutmeg
1/8 teaspoon cayenne pepper
1 1/2 cups water
1 1/2 cups coconut milk, fresh or canned,
   unsweetened

Prepare a roux by melting the butter in a skillet over medium heat and gradually adding the flour, stirring constantly. Cook for 3 to 5 minutes, then remove from the heat and set aside. The roux should resemble a paste.

In a large saucepan, place the pumpkin, christophene, eggplant, breadfruit, garlic, Scotch bonnet pepper, the 1 cup of shredded coconut, curry powder, salt, allspice, nutmeg, cayenne and water. Cook for 15 to 20 minutes over medium heat, stirring occasionally, until the vegetables are soft. Add the coconut milk and bring to a simmer. Stir in the roux, reduce the heat, and continue cooking for 2 minutes. Serve immediately over rice and top with remaining tablespoon of shredded coconut.

Yield: 4 main dish servings or 6 side-dish servings

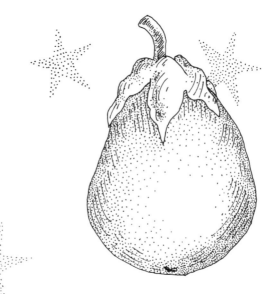

Sweet-and-Sour Vegetables

Pacific Rim

Sweet-and-sour sauces are another remnant of the Chinese influence throughout the South Pacific islands. When I was younger, I used to love chicken or shrimp in sweet-and-sour sauce, but I would always have a headache afterward. It turns out I wasn't alone; monosodium glutamate (MSG) often was added to the dish, and a lot of people had reactions to it. Of course, you won't find MSG anywhere in my kitchen, or in this book. Sweet-and-sour sauce is quite enticing without the dreaded additive.

Sauce

1/2 cup red wine vinegar
1/4 cup dry sherry
2 tablespoons soy sauce
2 tablespoons honey
1 tablespoon catsup

1 teaspoon cornstarch
1 teaspoon water
2 tablespoons peanut or vegetable oil
1 small onion, diced
1 red bell pepper, seeded and slivered
1 cup unpeeled, diced eggplant
6 to 8 broccoli florets
6 to 8 mushrooms, sliced
1/2 cup diced fresh pineapple
1 cup chopped bok choy
1 cup snow peas, ends removed
1 to 2 cloves garlic, minced
2 teaspoons minced fresh ginger
1 chile pepper, seeded and minced

To prepare the sauce, combine the vinegar, sherry, soy sauce, honey, and catsup in a mixing bowl. Set the sauce aside.

Combine the cornstarch and water in a small mixing bowl and set aside.

Heat the oil in a wok or large skillet. Add the onion, red pepper, eggplant, broccoli, mushrooms, and pine-apple. Stir fry for 3 to 4 minutes over medium heat. Add the bok choy, snow peas, garlic, ginger and chile pepper and continue to stir fry for another 2 minutes, until the vegetables are cooked but still firm.

Add the sauce to the vegetables in the wok and bring to a simmer, stirring occasionally. Simmer for 3 to 4 minutes. Stir in the cornstarch mixture and simmer for about 2 minutes more, stirring frequently. The mixture should thicken slightly and glisten. Serve immediately over rice.

Yield: 3 to 4 servings

Pumpkin Rice with Kale

West Indies

The calabaza pumpkin, also known as West Indian pumpkin, is a large, dark-green squash—so large that it is sold at street markets in wedges. Its golden orange flesh is similar to our big old jack-o-lantern pumpkins, but it tastes more like a butternut squash. Here it is stewed with rice, kale, and curry seasonings. This makes a versatile and nutritious side dish. If calabaza is unavailable, you may substitute butternut squash or a Halloween pumpkin.

2 tablespoons butter, melted
1 medium-size onion, diced
2 cups diced calabaza
1 Scotch bonnet pepper or 2 jalapeño peppers, seeded and minced
4 cloves garlic, minced
1 tablespoon fresh minced ginger
2 tablespoons curry powder
1 teaspoon Island Seasoning (page 25) or 1/2 teaspoon ground cloves and 1/2 teaspoon ground allspice
1 teaspoon ground cumin
1/2 teaspoon freshly ground black pepper
1/2 teaspoon salt
4 cups water
2 cups uncooked rice
2 cups chopped kale or spinach

Place the butter, onion, pumpkin, Scotch bonnet pepper, garlic, and ginger in a saucepan and saute for 7 to 10 minutes, until the vegetables are soft. Add the curry powder, Island Seasoning, cumin, black pepper, and salt and simmer for 1 minute more.

Add the water, rice, and kale, cover, and simmer over medium heat for 25 to 30 minutes, until the rice is fluffy. Serve immediately.

Yield: 6 to 8 servings

Pumpkin and Scallion Gratin

French West Indies

This recipe exemplifies the French influence on Caribbean cuisine. St. Martin, Guadeloupe, and Martinique are outposts of French cooking with an island twist.

4 tablespoons butter
2 tablespoons all-purpose flour
4 cups diced calabaza, pumpkin or butternut squash
2 to 3 cloves garlic, minced
1 Scotch bonnet pepper or jalapeño pepper, seeded and minced
2 cups chopped green onions (about 8 scallions)
1 cup coconut milk, fresh or canned, unsweetened
1/2 cup milk
1 tablespoon fresh thyme leaves (or 1/2 teaspoon dried thyme)
1/2 teaspoon ground allspice
1/2 teaspoon ground nutmeg
1/4 teaspoon salt
1/8 teaspoon cayenne pepper
1/4 cup bread crumbs

To make a roux, melt 2 tablespoons of the butter in a skillet over medium heat. Gradually blend in the flour, stirring frequently. Cook the paste for 4 to 5 minutes, but do not brown. Set aside.

Place the pumpkin in boiling water to cover and boil for about 5 minutes. Drain in a colander and cool slightly. Discard the water.

Preheat the oven to 375 degrees F.

Melt the remaining 2 tablespoons of butter in a saucepan. Add the garlic, chile peppers, and green onions, and saute for 5 to 7 minutes. Add the coconut milk, milk, thyme, allspice, nutmeg, salt, and cayenne. Cook over medium heat, stirring frequently, for 5 minutes, until the mixture almost simmers. Whisk in the roux and heat for another 2 minutes, continuing to stir.

Place the pumpkin in the bottom of a lightly greased baking or gratin dish. Pour the milk mixture over the pumpkin and sprinkle with the bread crumbs. Bake for 20 minutes. Serve immediately from the baking dish.

Yield: 4 to 6 servings

Fried Plantains

West Indies

Plantains, a Caribbean staple, have quickly become a popular side dish at my restaurant. They look like an overgrown banana, but even though they are in the banana family, they have to be cooked to be palatable. When plantains are green, they resemble a a potato in flavor and texture. As they ripen and turn yellow with patches of black, they become sweeter and softer. My favorite way to cook plantains is to fry them in a skillet and sprinkle ground cloves and nutmeg over them. Plantains are an excellent source of carbohydrates.

2 tablespoons butter
2 yellow plantains, peeled and sliced at an angle
** 1/4-inch thick**
1/4 teaspoon ground cloves
1/4 teaspoon ground nutmeg

Melt the butter in a large skillet and bring to a sizzle over moderately high heat. Add the plantains and sprinkle with half of the spices. After 4 or 5 minutes, turn the plantains and sprinkle with the remaining spices. Cook for another 4 minutes, until the plantains are golden brown.

Serve the plantains with Jamaican Jerk Chicken, Gabrielle Roasted Chicken, Calypso Steak, or by themselves with Tamarind-Pepper Sauce, Mango-Papaya Sauce, or Tomatillo Hot Sauce.

Yield: 4 servings

THE ART OF PEELING A PLANTAIN

Don't try to peel the plantains like a banana; it won't work. First, cut off the top and "tail." Next, make two or three slits lengthwise, but be careful not to cut into the flesh. Lift up the tip of the peel and run your thumb along lengthwise, pulling back and removing the peel. Now the plantains are ready to be sliced.

If you like sweet plantains, like me, it's a good idea to buy them a few days ahead of time, since green plantains need a few days to ripen. Always store plantains at room temperature; refrigeration makes them taste chalky.

Green Papaya Salad

Thailand

Thai papayas, when they are green and unripe, have the consistency and flavor of cabbage. They often are shredded and seasoned with spicy ingredients, creating a fiery equivalent of our cole slaw. This salad makes a savory accompaniment to Chicken Satay, Tamarind Lamb Satay, or Pineapple Barbecued Ribs.

1 cup shredded white cabbage
1 cup shredded green papaya or red cabbage
1/2 cup shredded carrot
2 to 3 chile peppers, seeded and minced
2 teaspoons minced fresh ginger
1 to 2 cloves garlic, minced
1/4 cup lime juice
3 tablespoons fish sauce or soy sauce
1 teaspoon hot sesame oil
1 teaspoon Dijon-style mustard
1 teaspoon brown sugar

Combine all of the ingredients in a large mixing bowl and toss thoroughly. Refrigerate for at least 1 hour before serving.

Yield: 4 servings

Rainbow Fruit Salad

Caribbean Islands

This colorful tropical salad is ideal for an early summer picnic, when many of these fruits are in season. For a special treat, serve the salad in a hollowed-out pineapple or papaya shell.

Cherimoya and starfruit are available in Caribbean markets.

1 cherimoya, seeded and pulp removed
1 papaya, peeled, seeded, and diced
1 mango, peeled, pitted, and diced
2 kiwifruit, peeled and diced
1 cup diced fresh pineapple
1 starfruit (carambola), sliced
1 cup plain or vanilla yogurt
1 tablespoon honey (optional)
1/2 teaspoon Island Seasoning (page 25)

Combine all of the ingredients in a large mixing bowl. Toss thoroughly. Serve immediately on a bed of leafy green lettuce or in a hollowed-out pineapple or papaya shell.

Yield: 4 to 5 servings

Condiments
& Sauces

Apricot-Fig Relish

Hawaii

When in Hawaii, I tasted apricots the size of large peaches. I also tried plump, chewy figs, a relative of the banana. Once considered rare and expensive, and only offered in the dried form, apricots and figs now have become more widely available on the mainland. I can even purchase apricots at the local farmer's market in the middle of summer. This is an adventurous relish to serve with lamb, pork, chicken, steamed vegetables or squash.

4 large or 6 small apricots, pitted and diced
1 cup chopped figs
1 medium-size onion, diced
3/4 cup red wine vinegar
1/4 cup brown sugar
2 to 3 cloves garlic, minced
1 tablespoon minced fresh ginger
1/2 teaspoon ground cloves
1/2 teaspoon freshly ground black pepper
1/2 teaspoon salt
1/4 cup fresh mint (optional)

Combine the apricots, figs, onion, vinegar, brown sugar, garlic, ginger, cloves, pepper, and salt in a nonreactive saucepan. Cook over medium heat for 10 minutes, stirring occasionally. Transfer to a serving bowl and stir in the mint leaves. Serve warm or refrigerate.

Yield: 2 cups

Banana and Kiwi Chutney

It's no secret that bananas are grown and sold throughout the tropics. However, their culinary versatility sometimes is overlooked. Aside from eating a banana almost every day for the past few years, I have used bananas for a variety of chutneys and relishes. Here they team up with kiwifruit to form a sweet-and-sour condiment for chicken, pork, fish, or lamb.

3 kiwifruit, peeled and sliced
2 bananas, peeled and sliced
1 cup diced red onion
3/4 cup red wine vinegar
1/4 cup brown sugar
2 to 3 cloves garlic, minced
2 teaspoons minced fresh ginger
1/4 teaspoon cayenne pepper
1/4 teaspoon ground allspice
1/4 teaspoon ground cloves
1/4 teaspoon salt

Combine all of the ingredients in a large, nonreactive saucepan and cook over low heat, stirring occasionally. Simmer for 12 to 15 minutes, until the mixture has a jam-like consistency.

Allow the chutney to cool to room temperature, then refrigerate. If refrigerated, the chutney should keep for 2 to 3 weeks.

Yield: 2 cups

Mango Salsa

Yucatan

One of the many culinary thrills in the tropics is the opportunity to indulge in fresh mangoes and papayas. On my visits, I would seek out street vendors offering the fruits, take the fruits back to the hotel, borrow a knife and spoon from the kitchen, and dig in. I would also enjoy mangoes and papayas first thing in the morning with a pot of strong coffee and the early sun breaking into the room. What decadence! Mangoes convey a variety of fruity flavors that range from pineapple to papaya and kiwi, from apple to lemony-lime. Mango, combined with the core flavors of salsa, lime juice, cilantro, and jalapeno peppers, yields a light condiment ideal for grilled fish and chicken.

1 ripe mango, peeled, pitted, and diced
1/4 cup minced red onion
1 Scotch bonnet pepper or jalapeño pepper, seeded and minced
2 tablespoons lime juice
1 tablespoon minced fresh cilantro
1/4 teaspoon ground cumin
1/4 teaspoon white pepper
1/4 teaspoon salt

Combine all of the ingredients in a bowl and mix thoroughly. Refrigerate for 1 hour. Serve with grilled fish, chicken, or lamb.

Yield: 2 cups

Mango-Papaya Sauce

West Indies

This is a sweet-and-tart dipping sauce. Serve it with chicken wings, vegetables, plantains, or fried fish.

1 mango, peeled, pitted, and diced
1 papaya, peeled, seeded, and diced
1 red onion, diced
1 cup red wine vinegar
1/4 cup brown sugar
1/4 cup raisins
2 to 3 cloves garlic, minced
2 teaspoons minced fresh ginger
1 teaspoon Island Seasoning (page 25)

Combine all of the ingredients in a large, nonreactive saucepan and cook over low heat, stirring occasionally. Simmer for 12 to 15 minutes, until the mixture has a jam-like consistency.

Allow the sauce to cool to room temperature. Place the mixture in a food processor fitted with a steel blade and process for 15 to 20 seconds. The sauce should be smooth, with only a few chunks. Serve immediately or refrigerate. If refrigerated, the sauce should keep for 2 to 3 weeks.

Yield: 2 cups

Papaya Mustard Sauce

West Indies

Papaya—also known as tree melon or pawpaw—has light green to coral-yellow skin, with pinkish-orange flesh. To enjoy a papaya, simply cut it in half and scoop out and discard the shiny black seeds. Ripe papayas are as soft as ripe avocados. Here the sweet, mellow, fruity flavor of papaya complements the heat of chile peppers and the pungency of mustard. Serve this sauce with grilled fish, chicken, or pork, or as an accompaniment to Plantain-Crusted Grouper, Citrus Grilled Ahi, or Chicharrones de Pollo.

1 papaya, peeled, seeded, and diced
1 tomato, diced
1/2 cup diced red onion
1 Scotch bonnet pepper or 2 jalapeño peppers,
  seeded and minced
1/2 cup red wine vinegar
1/4 cup dry white wine
2 tablespoons Dijon-style mustard
2 tablespoons brown sugar
2 tablespoons worcestershire sauce
1 teaspoon red hot sauce
1/2 teaspoon ground allspice
1/4 teaspoon white pepper
1/4 teaspoon salt

Combine all of the ingredients in a large, nonreactive saucepan and cook over low heat, stirring occasionally. Simmer for 10 to 12 minutes, until the mixture has a jam-like consistency.

Allow the sauce to cool to room temperature. Place the mixture in a food processor fitted with a steel blade and process for 15 to 20 seconds. The sauce should be smooth, with only a few chunks. Serve immediately or refrigerate. If refrigerated, the sauce should keep for about 2 weeks.

Yield: 2 cups

Indonesian Peanut Sauce

Indonesia

This is one of those sauces that people inevitable draw second and third helpings. It is traditionally served with satays, and also accompanies roast or grilled chicken, pork, or lamb. In addition, it makes a great vegetable dip, or a condiment for Chicken Satay. The combination of coconut, lime juice, and peanut butter, along with the Indonesian seasonings of coriander, cumin, and lemongrass will leave an indelible impression on your palate.

1 tablespoon peanut oil
1 medium-size onion, diced
2 cloves garlic, minced
1 chile pepper, seeded and minced
1 tablespoon minced fresh lemongrass
1/4 cup soy sauce, fish sauce, or ketjap manis
2 tablespoons brown sugar
2 tablespoons lime juice
1 1/2 cups coconut milk, fresh or canned, unsweetened
1 teaspoon ground coriander
1 teaspoon ground cumin
1 cup chunky peanut butter
1 tablespoon minced fresh cilantro

In a skillet, saute the peanut oil, onion, garlic, chile pepper, and lemongrass for about 4 minutes. Stir in the soy sauce, brown sugar, lime juice, coconut milk, coriander, and cumin. Thoroughly blend the peanut butter into the mixture. Bring the sauce to a simmer over low heat, stirring frequently. Stir in the cilantro and remove from the heat. Serve at once or refrigerate.

Yield: 2 cups

Lime-Peanut Dipping Sauce

Indonesia

Peanut butter combines with soy sauce, lime juice, ginger root, and chile peppers to form a very strong, complex taste. It has garnered kind of a cult following at my restaurant: Customers spread it on bread, spoon it over salad, even spread it on bananas. It makes a jazzy accompaniment to mildly flavored fish or chicken dishes, as well as satays.

1/2 cup crunchy, unsalted peanut butter
1/4 cup soy sauce or ketjap manis
3 tablespoons lime juice
2 teaspoons dark sesame oil
1/2 teaspoon hot oil
1/4 cup unsalted roasted peanuts
3 to 4 cloves garlic, minced
1 chile pepper, seeded and minced
1 teaspoon minced fresh ginger
1/4 teaspoon red pepper flakes

Combine all of the ingredients in a food processor fitted with a steel blade and process for 10 to 15 seconds, scraping the sides of the bowl at least once.

If blending by hand, fold the peanut butter into the rest of the ingredients until it is fully incorporated.

Serve at room temperature. If refrigerated, the sauce should keep for 2 to 3 weeks. Stir well before serving.

Yield: 1 cup

Groundnut Sauce

West Indies

The West African influence in the Caribbean islands led to a variety of groundnut pastes and sauces. (Groundnut is another name for the American peanut.) Traditionally, the groundnuts would be cracked, peeled, and crushed into a paste, but the wide availability of peanut butter has made that task unnecessary. This sauce is ideal for fish, meat, and vegetable dishes. I add it to sauteed chicken and vegetables and serve it over rice.

2 tablespoons butter, melted
1 medium-size onion, diced
2 tomatoes, diced
2 teaspoons minced fresh ginger
1 1/2 cups chunky peanut butter
3/4 cup water
2 tablespoons canned crushed tomato
1 teaspoon red pepper flakes
1/4 teaspoon ground allspice
1 teaspoon fresh thyme leaves or 1/4 teaspoon
    dried thyme
1/4 teaspoon freshly ground black pepper
1/4 teaspoon salt

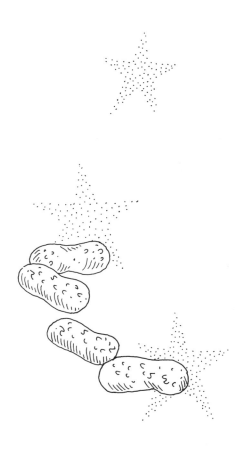

Place the butter, onion, tomatoes, and ginger in a saucepan and saute over medium heat for 7 to 10 minutes. Stir in the peanut butter, water, crushed tomatoes, and seasonings. Continue to cook for 5 to 10 minutes, stirring frequently. Remove from the heat and transfer to a serving bowl.

Yield: 3 cups

Creole Sauce

West Indies

Most Americans think Creole refers to a Louisiana style of cooking, but it also is a major element of Caribbean cuisine. The French, Spanish, Portuguese, English, Africans, Indians, and Caribs all contributed to the Caribbean version of Creole cooking. This sauce is one of my favorites: I spoon it over steaks, hamburgers, and grilled chicken, and add it to a variety of jambalayas (see Pork and Chicken Jambalaya).

1 tablespoon butter
1/2 tablespoon olive or other vegetable oil
1/2 small bell pepper, seeded and diced
1 small onion, diced
1 small tomato, diced
1/4 cup diced celery
1/4 cup chopped cooked okra
1 to 2 cloves garlic, minced
1 cup canned crushed tomatoes
1/4 cup plus 2 tablespoons water
1/8 cup dry red wine
1/2 tablespoon worcestershire sauce
1/2 tablespoon dried oregano
1 teaspoon dried parsley
1/2 to 1 teaspoon red hot sauce
1/4 teaspoon onion powder
1/4 teaspoon salt
1/8 teaspoon freshly ground black pepper
1/8 teaspoon white pepper
1/8 teaspoon cayenne pepper
1/8 teaspoon red pepper flakes

Heat the butter and oil in a saucepan. Add the bell pepper, onion, fresh tomato, celery, okra, and garlic and saute over moderately high heat for 10 to 12 minutes, stirring occasionally. Reduce the heat to medium after about 5 minutes. The vegetables should be slightly cooked and still firm.

Reduce the heat to low and add the remaining ingredients to the pan. Bring the sauce to a simmer and continue to cook for 15 to 20 minutes, stirring frequently.

Serve the sauce immediately or refrigerate. If refrigerated, the sauce should keep for 7 to 10 days.

Yield: 2 1/4 cups

Tomatillo Hot Sauce

One of my priorities upon arriving on a tropical island is to sample the local hot sauces. Many of the islands boast their own special ingredients and brewing techniques. With this island spirit in mind, I created a green sauce with tart tomatillos and fiery chile peppers. Tomatillos, also known as green tomatoes, are as tart as a young, green apple. Because of their sour, almost lime-like taste, they often are juxtaposed with more biting flavors, such as hot chile peppers and cilantro. They are an ideal medium for extra-spicy sauces. Serve this version as you would bottled hot sauces or mustard.

6 medium-size tomatillos or 6 small green
   tomatoes, diced
2 to 3 chile peppers, seeded and minced
3/4 cup red wine vinegar
1/2 cup diced red onion
1/4 cup brown sugar
1 tablespoon minced fresh cilantro
1 to 2 teaspoons red hot sauce
1/2 teaspoon white pepper
1/2 teaspoon black pepper
1/4 teaspoon salt

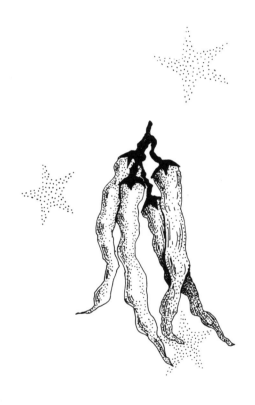

Combine all of the ingredients in a nonreactive saucepan and bring to a simmer over medium heat. Simmer for 20 minutes, stirring occasionally. Remove from the heat and puree the mixture for 30 seconds in a food processor fitted with a steel blade or blender.

Serve immediately or wrap and chill. If refrigerated, the sauce should keep for 7 days.

Yield: 1 1/2 cups

Sofrito

Spanish West Indies

Sofrito is a condiment carried to the Caribbean islands by Spanish settlers. The tomato-based sauce is similar to Creole sauce, only milder. Islanders spoon sofrito over peas and rice, soup, stew, chicken, pork, beef, and even vegetables. Annatto liquid gives the sauce a vibrant reddish-orange hue. Annatto liquid is available in Caribbean food shops. If unavailable, substitute a small pinch of turmeric or saffron.

1 tablespoon butter or lard
1/4 pound salt pork, diced
1 bell pepper, seeded and finely chopped
1 tomato, diced
1 medium-size onion, diced
1 clove garlic, minced
1 teaspoon annatto liquid
2 tablespoons crushed canned tomato
2 tablespoons water
2 teaspoons minced fresh cilantro
1/2 teaspoon freshly ground black pepper

Place the butter and salt pork in a skillet and saute for about 10 minutes over medium heat, until the pork has rendered most of its liquid. Remove the salt pork and discard, but save the rendered fat. Add the bell pepper, tomato, onion, garlic, and annatto liquid and saute for 6 to 8 minutes. Add the crushed tomatoes, water, cilantro, and black pepper and simmer for 3 to 5 minutes, stirring frequently.

Remove from the heat and serve immediately, or refrigerate.

Yield: 1 cup

Tamarind Pepper Sauce

Trinidad

Tamarind is a pea-shaped pod with a firm, sour flesh. It is often used in soups, stews, or sweetened drinks. When fresh tamarind is unavailable, the dry, crushed pod can be substituted: Simply reconstitute the pod in water, then extract and drain the stock. Tamarind is also occasionally available in a potent paste. The flavor is a cross between a herbal tea and a prune. It combines well with the sweet, sour, and hot flavors of sugar, vinegar, and chile peppers.

1 cup warm water
4 ounces dried tamarind
2 to 3 Scotch bonnet peppers or 4 to 6 jalapeño peppers, seeded and minced
2 tomatoes, diced
1 mango, peeled, pitted and diced
1 medium-size onion, diced
2 to 3 cloves garlic, minced
3/4 cup red wine vinegar
1/4 cup brown sugar
14 to 16 allspice berries, crushed
1/2 teaspoon ground cloves
1/2 teaspoon ground nutmeg
1/2 teaspoon salt

Combine the water and dried tamarind and set aside for 1 to 2 hours, stirring occasionally. Drain the mixture through a sieve. Save the tamarind liquid and discard the pulp. (If you are using tamarind paste, mix 2 tablespoons of the paste with 3/4 cup of water).

Combine the tamarind liquid with the peppers, tomatoes, mango, onion, garlic, vinegar, brown sugar, and seasonings in a nonreactive saucepan and cook over medium heat, stirring occasionally. Cook for 25 to 30 minutes, until the sauce is thick and chunky. Remove the sauce from the heat and set aside for 10 minutes. Place the sauce in a food processor fitted with a steel blade and process for 20 to 30 seconds, until the sauce is smooth. Serve the sauce with sauteed scallops, shrimp, chicken, pork, or steamed vegetables.

Yield: 3 cups

Sambal

Indonesia

Sambal is a piquant relish served with Indonesian meals. Although chile peppers are the main thrust of this condiment, a variety of other ingredients—such as eggplant, tuna, coconut milk, and macadamia nuts—can be included. (See Wok-Seared Tuna with Pineapple Sambal.)

1 tablespoon peanut or vegetable oil
6 to 8 chile peppers, seeded and diced
2 tablespoons minced shallots
2 teaspoons brown sugar
1/4 cup red wine vinegar

Heat the oil in a saucepan. Add the chile peppers, shallots, and brown sugar. Saute for 3 to 4 minutes over medium heat. Reduce the heat, add the vinegar, and cook for about 7 minutes, until most of the vinegar has evaporated. Remove from the heat and cool to room temperature. Serve immediately or refrigerate. If refrigerated, the sambal should keep for 2 to 3 weeks.

Yield: 1/2 cup

Variations

To make Eggplant Sambal, saute 1 cup diced eggplant and 1 diced tomato with the chile peppers, and add 1/4 cup more vinegar and 1 tablespoon more brown sugar. For Coconut Sambal, saute 1 small diced onion with the chile pepper and substitute 1/2 cup coconut milk (fresh or canned, unsweetened), 2 tablespoons lime juice, and 1 tablespoon minced fresh cilantro in place of the vinegar.

Starfruit Relish

West Indies

Starfruit, also known as carambola, is a crisp, moist fruit with a ribbed, oblong shape. When sliced crosswise, the fruit yields photogenic, star-shaped slices. When the fruit is green, it is mouth-puckering tart, but as it ripens to yellow, it becomes sweet and refreshing. When the weather gets extremely hot, a starfruit is thirst-quenching. Although starfruit often is relegated to the role of a cute garnish at fancy restaurants, its flavor and texture warrant a variety of culinary uses. Here the fruit forms a tangy relish, ideal with pork, chicken, or lamb.

2 yellow starfruit, sliced
1 medium-size red onion, sliced
1 apple, unpeeled and sliced
1 cup red wine vinegar
1/2 cup raisins
1/4 cup brown sugar
1/2 teaspoon ground cloves
1/2 teaspoon ground nutmeg
1/4 teaspoon freshly ground black pepper
1/4 teaspoon salt

Combine all of the ingredients in a large, nonreactive saucepan and cook over low heat, stirring occasionally. Simmer for 15 to 20 minutes. Serve the relish immediately or refrigerate. If refrigerated, the relish should keep for 2 to 3 weeks.

Yield: 2 cups

Tropical Fruit Chutney

When I prepare this chutney for my cooking classes, students wolf it down as if it were a meal in itself. Pineapples, mangoes, papayas, and kiwifruit combine to form a delicious condiment. This chutney adds flair and flavor to any meal.

1 cup diced fresh pineapple
1 mango, peeled, pitted, and diced
1 papaya, peeled, seeded, and diced
1 medium-size red onion, diced
2 to 3 cloves garlic, minced
1 tablespoon minced fresh ginger
1 cup red wine vinegar
1/4 cup brown sugar
1/2 teaspoon ground cloves
1/2 teaspoon ground cumin
1/2 teaspoon freshly ground black pepper
1/4 teaspoon salt
1 kiwifruits, peeled and diced

Place all of the ingredients, except the kiwifruit, in a non-reactive saucepan and cook over medium heat. Simmer for 15 minutes, stirring occasionally. Lower the heat as the mixture begins to thicken. Stir in the kiwifruit and cook for another 5 minutes.

Allow the chutney to cool to room temperature, then refrigerate. If refrigerated, the chutney should keep for about 2 weeks.

Yield: 2 1/2 cups

Tropical Fruit Vinaigrette

I discovered fruit vinaigrettes while doing research for my first cookbook, *Condiments!* I was developing a recipe for chutney and pondering a new dressing for my restaurant when I shifted gears and made the mixture into a vinaigrette. The concept is simple: Simmer the fruit in vinegar, puree the batch in a food processor, and slowly drizzle in oil, thus creating the vinaigrette. Tropical fruits make excellent vinaigrettes, and they provide zest and color to tossed salads or steamed vegetables. Some customers at my restaurant liked this dressing so much that they purchased cups of it to take home with them.

1 papaya, seeded, peeled, and diced
1 mango, peeled, pitted, and diced
1 kiwifruit, peeled and diced
1 cup diced fresh pineapple
1 1/2 cups red wine vinegar
1/8 cup honey
1/4 teaspoon salt
1/4 teaspoon white pepper
1 to 1 1/4 cups vegetable oil

Place the papaya, mango, kiwifruit, pineapple, and vinegar in a nonreactive saucepan and cook for 5 to 7 minutes over medium heat. Refrigerate the mixture for about 30 minutes.

Place the fruit mixture, honey, and seasonings in a food processor fitted with a steel blade. Process for 20 to 30 seconds, until the mixture is smooth. Drizzle in the oil while the motor is running, and then process for 15 to 20 seconds more. Serve the dressing immediately or refrigerate. If refrigerated, the vinaigrette should keep for 1 to 2 weeks.

Yield: about 4 cups

Breads
& Desserts

Chile Pepper Corn Bread

Here's a cornbread with a kick to it. For a delightful and light meal, serve the bread with Chicken and Noodle Soup, Callabo, or Yuca and Tomato Stew.

1 cup yellow cornmeal
1 cup all-purpose flour
1/4 cup sugar
1 tablespoon baking powder
1/2 teaspoon salt
1 teaspoon coarsely crushed black peppercorns
2 eggs, beaten
1/2 cup buttermilk
1/2 cup milk
1/4 cup melted butter
1/2 cup chopped green onions
2 to 3 chile peppers, seeded and minced

Preheat the oven to 375 F.

Place the cornmeal, flour, sugar, baking powder, salt, and peppercorns in a bowl and stir together well. In a separate bowl, whisk together the eggs, buttermilk, milk, and melted butter. Add the green onions and peppers to the milk mixture.

Gently fold the liquid ingredients into the dry ingredients until the mixture forms a batter.

Pour the batter into a greased 8-inch square baking pan.

Bake for 20 to 25 minutes, until the crust is lightly browned and a toothpick inserted in the center comes out clean.

Cut into squares and serve at once.

Yield: 4 to 6 servings

Christophene-Carrot Bread

West Indies

Christophene, also known as chayote and cho-cho, is a pale green, gnarled, pear-shaped squash. The firm, moist flesh is ideal for soups, stuffing, vegetable dishes, stir-fries, and breads. Here I've shredded it and created a bread similar to zucchini bread. It's extremely moist. Be careful. You'll want to eat the entire batch.

1 1/4 cups oil
1 1/2 cups sugar
3 eggs
1 teaspoon vanilla extract
2 cups grated christophene or zucchini
1 cup grated carrot
2 cups all-purpose flour
2 teaspoons baking soda
1 teaspoon baking powder
1 teaspoon salt
1 teaspoon ground cinnamon
1 teaspoon ground nutmeg

Preheat the oven to 350 degrees F.

Whisk together the oil and sugar in a mixing bowl. Add the eggs, one at a time, and continue whisking until the batter is creamy. Fold in the remaining ingredients. Blend well. Pour the batter into 12 mini-loaf pans and bake for about 25 minutes, until a toothpick inserted in the center comes out clean. Serve immediately.

Yield: 12 small loaves

Coconut-Macadamia Bread

Hawaii

The macademia is the Rolls-Royce of nuts. Grown commercially on the volcanic Big Island of Hawaii, these waxy, cream-colored nuts exude a rich, lightly toasted flavor. Macadamia nuts—especially the chocolate-covered versions—have become a tasty souvenir for millions of visitors to Hawaii.

The candlenut, which grows in Southeast Asia and Indonesia, is similar to the macadamia. (Walnuts or cashews may be substituted for macadamia nuts in most recipes.)

2 cups all-purpose flour
1 1/2 cups shredded fresh coconut
1/2 cup chopped macadamia nuts or walnuts
1/2 cup sugar
2 teaspoons baking powder
1 teaspoon salt
1 teaspoon ground allspice
1 teaspoon ground nutmeg
1 teaspoon ground cloves
2 eggs, beaten
1/2 cup coconut milk, fresh or canned,
    unsweetened, or buttermilk
1/2 cup melted butter

Preheat oven to 350 degrees F.

In a large mixing bowl, combine the flour, coconut, nuts, sugar, baking powder, salt, allspice, nutmeg, and cloves. In a separate bowl, whisk together the eggs, coconut milk, and butter. Fold the liquid ingredients into the dry ingredients. Blend the mixture thoroughly.

Pour the mixture into a lightly greased 9-inch-by-5-inch loaf pan. Bake for 45 to 50 minutes, until a toothpick inserted in the center comes out clean. Place the bread on a rack and allow to cool slightly.

Serve with Jamaican Squash Bisque, Sweet Plantain and Saffron-Scented Soup, or Groundnut Stew.

Yield: 4 to 6 servings

Maui Onion Bread

Hawaii

The island of Maui is a short flight from Honolulu. (The flights are referred to as "puddle-jumpers," but the ride actually is very smooth.) Maui is less developed than Oahu, but the quaint resort towns of Ka'anapali and Lahaina bustle with the arts, water sports, and nightlife that are reminiscent of Cape Cod in the summertime. Maui is also known for the Kula variety of onion, or Maui onion, which grows on the high slopes of the "upcountry." Before I visited Maui, I thought onions were essentially a homogeneous lot. Then I tasted a big Maui onion; it was sharp, crisp, and sweet. The Maui onion inspired this moist and hearty quick bread.

2 cups diced sweet potatoes
1 cup all-purpose flour
1/2 cup whole wheat flour
2 teaspoons baking powder
1 teaspoon baking soda
1 teaspoon salt
1 teaspoon dried thyme
1 teaspoon black pepper
1/2 cup butter, softened
1/2 cup brown sugar
2 eggs
1/2 cup milk
1 Maui onion, minced

Preheat the oven to 350 degrees F.

Place the sweet potatoes in boiling water to cover and cook for 10 minutes, until the potatoes are tender. Drain the potatoes in a colander and cool under running cold water. Discard the water. Mash the potatoes with a fork until smooth. Set aside.

In a mixing bowl, combine all of the dry ingredients.

In a separate bowl, cream the butter. Cream in the brown sugar. Blend in the eggs, one at a time. Stir in the milk and onion. Add the mashed potatoes and blend until smooth. Gradually fold in the dry ingredient mixture.

Pour the dough into two lightly greased 8-inch-by-4-inch loaf pans. Bake for 25 minutes, until a toothpick inserted in the center comes out clean. Serve warm.

Yield: 6 to 8 servings

Pumpkin-Mango Muffins

Here's a muffin that can be served for breakfast, lunch, or dinner. These two native tropical ingredients create a quintessential 1990s muffin—flavorful, healthful, and quick and easy to prepare.

2 cups all-purpose flour
1 teaspoon salt
1 teaspoon ground cinnamon
1/2 teaspoon ground allspice
1/2 teaspoon baking soda
3 teaspoons baking powder
1/2 cup butter, softened
1/2 cup brown sugar, firmly packed
1/2 cup granulated sugar
2 eggs
1 cup cooked, mashed pumpkin
1/2 cup buttermilk
2 mangoes, peeled, pitted, and diced

Preheat the oven to 375 degrees F.

In a large mixing bowl, combine the flour, salt, cinnamon, allspice, baking soda, and baking powder.

In a separate mixing bowl, cream the butter. Add the brown sugar and white sugar to the butter and cream at high speed. Add the eggs, one at a time, and cream again. Add the mashed pumpkin and buttermilk and mix well. Stir in the mangoes.

Gently fold the dry ingredients into the pumpkin batter. Spoon the batter into greased muffin tins. Bake for about 20 minutes, until a toothpick inserted in the center comes out clean. After 10 minutes, remove the muffins from the pan and allow to cool on a rack.

Yield: 12 muffins

Jamaican Black Cake

Jamaica

This is a spin on fruitcake, but unlike the fruitcakes that travel around our country every holiday season, Jamaican black cakes are actually eaten. The name comes from the cake's dark color, due mostly to the burnt-sugar coloring found in Caribbean kitchens. The coloring can be made easily (see below) or purchased at a West Indian grocery. Molasses can be substituted with no loss of flavor, although it will make the cake dark brown, not black. The cake usually is served 2 to 3 days after it has been baked, but it can be hard to resist right out of the oven. Jamaican black cake is perfect for a morning or afternoon snack.

2 cups mixed dried fruit
1 cup plus 2 tablespoons dark rum
1/2 cup dark beer
1/2 pound butter, softened
1/2 cup brown sugar
1/4 cup granulated sugar
3 large eggs
1 teaspoon vanilla extract
1/2 teaspoon ground nutmeg
1/2 teaspoon ground allspice
2 tablespoons burnt-sugar coloring (see below)
1 cup all-purpose flour
1 teaspoon baking powder

Cover the dried fruit with 1 cup of the rum and the dark beer and set aside for 4 hours or overnight.

Preheat the oven to 350 degrees F.

Place the fruit mixture in a food processor fitted with a steel blade and process for 10 to 15 seconds, forming a pulp. Set aside.

In a mixing bowl, cream the butter with the brown and white sugar. Beat in the eggs, one at a time. Mix in the vanilla, nutmeg, allspice, and burnt-sugar coloring.

In a separate bowl, sift together the flour and baking powder. Gently fold, alternately, the fruit pulp and the dry ingredients into the batter.

Pour the batter into a shallow 9-inch-diameter greased cake pan and bake for 45 minutes to 1 hour, until a toothpick inserted in the center comes out clean.

While the cake is still warm, drizzle the remaining rum over the top. The cake is best served cool, even a day or two after baking.

Yield: one 9-inch round cake

Note: To make the burnt-sugar coloring, caramelize 1/4 cup granulated sugar in a heavy saucepan. Add 1/4 cup boiling water and remove from the heat. Combine thoroughly. The coloring will keep for several weeks in the refrigerator.

Pineapple Coconut Crisp

Here is a dessert that will make people gather round as soon as it comes out of the oven. The pineapple, coconut, and oatmeal combine to form a crunchy, tropical version of America's apple crisp. When buying a ripe pineapple, look for one that has a sweet aroma and a yellowish-brownish skin with a trace of green. The crown should be green and shiny, without splotches of brown.

Filling

6 cups diced fresh pineapple
2 tablespoons lemon juice
2 tablespoons honey
1/2 teaspoon ground cinnamon
1/2 teaspoon ground nutmeg

Topping

2 1/4 cups shredded fresh coconut
1/2 cup quick-cooking rolled oats
1 cup all-purpose flour
1/2 cup brown sugar
1/2 teaspoon ground cinnamon
1/3 cup butter or margarine, softened

Preheat the oven to 350 degrees F. Lightly grease a 2 1/2 - 3 quart casserole.

To prepare the filling, combine the pineapple, lemon juice, honey, cinnamon, and nutmeg in a mixing bowl. Spread the fruit mixture evenly in the bottom of the baking dish.

To prepare the topping, combine 2 cups of the coconut, the oats, flour, brown sugar, and cinnamon in a large mixing bowl. Cut the butter into the mixture until it resembles coarse meal. Sprinkle the topping evenly over the pineapple mixture. Sprinkle the remaining 1/4 cup of coconut over the top.

Bake for 20 to 25 minutes, until the pineapple is tender and the topping is browned. Serve warm with vanilla yogurt spooned over the top.

Yield: 6 to 8 servings

Mango Cobbler

When the tropics meet New England, you get mango cobbler. The fruity flavor and firm texture of a mango make it an ideal ingredient for baked desserts such as cobblers. This is especially good served with a dollop of Nutmeg and Coffee Ice Cream.

2 mangoes, peeled, pitted, and sliced
2 tablespoons lime juice
1/2 teaspoon ground nutmeg
1 cup all-purpose flour
2 teaspoons baking powder
1/4 teaspoon salt
1/2 cup brown sugar
3 tablespoons margarine, softened
1/2 cup whole or skim milk

Preheat the oven to 375 degrees F.

Combine the mangoes, lime juice, and nutmeg in a mixing bowl. Spoon the fruit into a lightly greased 8-inch square baking pan. To make the topping, combine the flour, baking powder, salt, and brown sugar in a mixing bowl. With a knife and fork, or a pastry cutter, cut the margarine into the flour until the mixture resembles coarse meal. Stir in the milk and blend the batter until it is smooth.

Spread the batter evenly over the all the fruit. Bake the cobbler for 20 to 25 minutes, until it is lightly browned on top. Allow to cool for a few minutes, then cut. Serve with yogurt, ice cream, or whipped cream spooned over the top.

Yield: 4 to 6 servings

Kiwi and Mango Flambe

2 tablespoons butter
2 tablespoons brown sugar
2 kiwifruit, peeled and sliced
1 mango, peeled, pitted, and sliced
1/8 teaspoon ground cinnamon
1/4 cup dark rum
1/4 cup creme de banana
1 pint vanilla or mint chocolate chip ice cream

Combine the butter and brown sugar in a skillet and cook over medium heat until the mixture turns to a syrup (about 3 minutes). Add the kiwifruit and mango slices and the cinnamon to the pan and saute for 3 minutes. Coat all of the slices thoroughly with the syrup. Add the rum and creme de banana and touch a match to the liqueur. Allow the flame to subside and continue cooking for 2 more minutes.

Scoop the ice cream into serving bowls, spoon the fruit over the ice cream, and devour at once.

Yield: 4 servings

Bananas Flambe

West Indies

Here is the finishing touch for my cooking classes on tropical cuisine. I conclude the class by turning down the lights, flambeing the bananas, and serving them over frozen yogurt. Everyone goes wild. I also immediately hand out the instructor evaluation forms at that point, getting them while they're in a cheerful mood.

This is an exquisite way to devour bananas. If you are a banana lover, like me, you will especially relish this classic yet simple dessert.

2 tablespoons butter
2 tablespoons brown sugar
4 bananas, peeled and sliced crosswise
1/4 teaspoon ground cinnamon
1/4 cup dark rum
1/4 cup creme de banana
1 pint vanilla or chocolate ice cream or frozen yogurt

Combine the butter and brown sugar in a skillet and cook over medium heat until the mixture forms a syrup (about 3 minutes). Add the banana slices and cinnamon to the pan and saute for 3 minutes. Turn the slices gently to coat them thoroughly with the syrup. Add the rum and creme de banana and touch a match to the liqueur. Allow the flame to subside and continue cooking for 1 more minute.

Scoop the ice cream into serving bowls, spoon the bananas over the ice cream, and dig in.

Yield: 4 servings

Watermelon and Mango Mousse

Watermelon is the quintessential tropical fruit—sweet, juicy, and easily devoured. Split the watermelon and pass the napkins. Watermelon connoisseurs test for ripeness by thumping the fruit with their fingers, listening for a hollow thud.

Here the summery flavor of watermelon teams up with another quintessential tropical fruit, mango, to form a light and refreshing mousse.

1 envelope unflavored gelatin
2 tablespoons hot water
2 ripe mangoes, peeled, pitted, and diced
2 cups seeded, diced watermelon
Juice of 1 lime
2 tablespoons sugar
3 egg whites
1/4 teaspoon salt
1/2 cup heavy cream
1/2 teaspoon ground nutmeg

In a small bowl, dissolve the gelatin in the hot water. Set aside.

Place the mangoes in a food processor fitted with a steel blade and process for 20 to 30 seconds. Add the watermelon, lime juice, sugar, and gelatin and process for another 20 seconds.

In a mixing bowl, beat the egg whites with the salt, until the whites hold a peak.

In a separate bowl, whip the heavy cream vigorously until it is thick and stiff.

Fold the watermelon-mango puree into the egg whites. Gradually fold in the whipped cream. Pour into 6 tulip-shaped glasses and refrigerate for 2 to 3 hours, until the mousse is firm. Sprinkle the nutmeg over the mousse before serving. Garnish with a mint sprig.

Yield: 6 servings

Nutmeg and Coffee Ice Cream

The tropics are known for robust coffee plants, especially Jamaica's Blue Mountain and Hawaii's Kona varieties. The coffee beans also are processed into coffee liqueurs, which, in turn, transform a variety of beverages and desserts. For a delicious ice cream and a real island treat, this recipe teams up nutmeg with coffee liqueur.

1 1/2 tablespoons ground nutmeg or allspice
2 cups heavy cream
2 cups light cream
3/4 cup sugar
1/4 cup coffee liqueur

Combine all of the ingredients in a mixing bowl. Beat until the sugar dissolves. Freeze according to the directions on the ice cream maker.

Yield: about 1 1/2 quarts

Haupia, Coconut Pudding

Hawaii

Haupia is the classic dessert served at a Hawaiian luau. But you don't have to attend a luau to indulge in haupia —it's quick and quite easy to make.

1/4 cup sugar
1/4 cup cornstarch
1 1/2 cups coconut milk, fresh or canned, unsweetened
1 tablespoon vanilla extract

Combine the sugar and cornstarch in a small bowl and set aside. Place the coconut milk and vanilla in a saucepan and cook over low heat for 4 to 5 minutes, stirring frequently. Whisk the dry ingredients into the coconut milk and simmer for 3 to 4 minutes, stirring frequently until the mixture thickens.

Pour the pudding into an 8-inch square pan and refrigerate for about 2 hours, until the pudding is firm. Cut into squares and serve as a dessert for any tropical meal.

Yield: 6 to 8 servings

Drinks

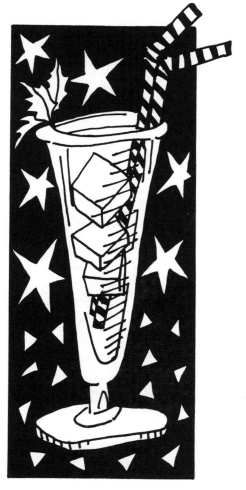

Coconut Water

Coconut water is the liquid that sloshes around inside the coconut when you shake it. While green coconuts are prized for their water, the more common brown coconut also yields a rich beverage. Although there is a strong temptation to insert a straw into the coconut and drink the liquid straight from the shell, it's always a good idea first to strain the water.

1 coconut

Pierce the "eyes" of the coconut with an ice pick. Set the coconut over a sturdy glass and allow to drain. Strain the water and pour into a glass filled with ice. Drink immediately.

Yield: 1 serving

Ginger Beer

West Indies

Homemade ginger beer is a traditional West Indies beverage. Although it is referred to as a beer, it is closer to a carbonated soda with a strong ginger flavor.

1/2 cup grated ginger
4 cups boiling water
Juice of 1 lime
1 cup sugar
1/2 teaspoon dried yeast

Combine all of the ingredients except the yeast and stir. Let cool to 96 degrees F. Add the yeast and stir. Place in a large container. Seal tightly and store at room temperature for at least 24 hours. Strain and refrigerate until well chilled.

Yield: 4 servings

Tropical Smoothie

Here is a refreshing, fruity shake ideal for a morning breakfast on the patio.

1 mango, peeled, pitted and diced
1 papaya, peeled, seeded and diced
1 kiwifruit, peeled and diced
1 banana, peeled and diced
1 cup lowfat plain or vanilla yogurt
1/8 teaspoon ground cloves

Combine the mango, papaya, kiwifruit, banana, and yogurt in a blender and blend until smooth. Pour into a large glass and sprinkle with cloves.

Yield: 4 servings

Tamarinade

I first tasted this refreshing beverage in Jamaica, where the Tamarind tree grows large and abundantly. You'll find versions of this drink throughout the Caribbean as well as India and Southeast Asia.

15 to 20 tamarind pods or 1 cup tamarind pulp
1 cup brown sugar
1 tablespoon freshly grated ginger root
6 cups warm water
Cold water, to taste
Brown or white sugar, to taste
8 orange slices, for garnish

You will find both the fresh pod and the canned pulp in most Hispanic and Caribbean food stores. If using the pods, remove the long thin outer shell. Combine the pods or canned pulp with the 1 cup brown sugar and grated ginger root and soak in warm water for 45 minutes. Strain and push the pulp through a strainer with a spoon or pestle. Discard the seeds and membrane remaining. The remaining mixture will be extremely tart. Add cold water and sugar to taste. Chill and serve in tall glasses with ice cubes garnished with oranges slices. For an interesting touch add a small amount of baking soda to each glass just before serving to add "fizziness."

Yield: 6 to 8 servings

Tamarind Iced Tea

The tea-like flavor of tamarind makes it a favorite ingredient for a cold drink throughout the tropics. Fresh mint adds an herbal touch.

2 teaspoons tamarind concentrate
1 teaspoon honey
1 cup cold water
Mint leaves, for garnish

Combine all of the ingredients in a tall glass and stir thoroughly. Pour into a tall glass filled with ice and garnish with a sprig of mint leaves.

Yield: 1 serving

Sorrel Drink

Sorrel is a traditional drink served at Christmas time. Legend has it that the sorrel plant will yield its red flowers just before Christmas regardless of when it was planted. You will be able to find fresh sorrel in food stores in early December. While fresh is the best, you can use dried sorrel which is available year-round.

3 dozen fresh sorrel sepals or 2 ounces dried sorrel
1/2 cup freshly grated ginger
1/4 cup lime juice
2 cups brown or white sugar
2 quarts boiling water

If using fresh sorrel, peel off the red sepals and discard the buds. Combine the red sepals or dried sorrel with the ginger and lime juice in a large bowl. Pour the boiling water over the mixture, cover, and steep overnight (it does not need to be refrigerated). Strain out the solids and sweeten with sugar to taste. Chill and serve in cocktail glasses over cracked ice or in a punch bowl with ice, cut lemons and limes.

Yield: 2 1/2 quarts

The Grand Banana

This is a great use for overripe bananas that you can't stand to turn into yet another banana bread.

6 to 8 ripe bananas, peeled
1 can condensed milk
1/2 cup brown sugar
2 scoops vanilla ice cream
1 cup ice cubes

In a blender, combine the bananas with condensed milk, brown sugar, vanilla ice cream, and ice cubes. Blend until smooth. Serve in a tall glass.

Yield: 4 servings

Golden Piña Colada

Every resort and bar in the world must serve a pina colada. I couldn't resist the challenge to present a variation of this well-known concoction. As tacky as it may sound, I recommend investing in some of those tiny paper umbrellas to garnish the drink with.

3 tablespoons dark rum
1 tablespoon Galliano
1/8 cup cream of coconut (Coco Lopes makes a good brand)
1/4 cup pineapple, freshly cut and ripe is the best, canned will do
1/8 cup lime juice
1 cup ice cubes
1 tablespoon shredded coconut
1 pineapple spear, for garnish
1 paper umbrella, for garnish

In a blender, combine the rum, Galliano, cream of coconut, pineapple, lime juice, and ice cubes. Blend mixture about 2 minutes, and pour into a tall glass. Top with shredded coconut, and garnish with a pineapple spear and the paper umbrella.

Yield: 1 serving

Mango Colada

St. Martins

This is truly one of the best colada drinks you will ever indulge in. I was introduced to the mango colada in St. Martin, and it has remained my favorite drink ever since.

3 tablespoons dark rum
1/2 cup pineapple juice
1/2 cup cream of coconut
1 cup crushed ice
1 mango, peeled, pitted and diced
1 whole nutmeg
1 maraschino cherry, for garnish

Combine the rum, pineapple juice, cream of coconut, ice, and mango in a blender and blend until smooth. Pour into a tall glass and grate the nutmeg over the top. Garnish with a maraschino cherry.

Yield: 3 to 4 servings

Denny's Margarita

1/3 cup tequila
1/4 cup Triple Sec or Cointreau
1/4 cup lime juice
1 cup ice cubes
2 lime wedges, for garnish

In a blender, combine the tequila, Triple Sec, lime juice, and ice cubes. Blend until smooth. Pour into margarita glasses (with salted rims, if you wish), and garnish with lime wedges.

Yield: 2 servings

Blue Hawaii

This exotic-looking, sprightly flavored drink exemplifies the fun-in-the-sun spirit of the tropics.

1/8 cup white rum
1 tablespoon blue curacao
1/4 cup pineapple juice
1 tablespoon lime juice
1/8 cup simple sugar (see below)
1 cup ice cubes
1 pineapple wedge, for garnish
1 maraschino cherry, for garnish
1 paper umbrella, for garnish

Combine all of the ingredients in a blender and blend until smooth. Pour into a tall glass and garnish with a pineapple wedge, maraschino cherry, and funky umbrella.

Yield: 1 serving

Goombay Smash

The Goombay Festival in the Bahamas is a yearly carnival-like celebration, and this drink is the official libation.

1/8 cup dark rum
1/8 cup light rum
1/2 cup pineapple juice
2 ounces cream of coconut
1 lime wedge, for garnish
1 maraschino cherry, for garnish

In a mixing glass, combine all of the ingredients and shake well. Pour into a glass filled with ice, and garnish with a lime wedge and maraschino cherry.

Yield: 1 serving

To make the simple sugar, combine 1/2 cup water and 1/2 cup sugar in a saucepan and bring to a boil, stirring to dissolve the sugar. Reduce the heat and simmer for 2 to 3 minutes. Remove from the heat and allow to cool to room temperature. The syrup will keep for several weeks if tightly wrapped and refrigerated.

Bajan Rum Punch

1/8 cup dark rum
1/4 cup pineapple juice
1/4 cup orange juice
1 tablespoon lemon juice
1/8 teaspoon Angostura bitters

    In a mixing bowl, combine all of the ingredients and shake well. Pour into a tall glass filled with ice and garnish with a lime wedge.

Yield: 1 serving

Papaya Apricot Daiquiri

Legend has it that Earnest Hemingway had something to do with the invention of the daiquiri during his adventures in Cuba. (Given his propensity for drinking, the story is not entirely far fetched.) Another legend is that daiquiri is the name of a town in Cuba, and workers ended their work day with a rum-slush-fruit concoction. The rest is history: Every fruit in the world at one time or another has been made into a daiquiri.

1/8 cup rum
1 tablespoon apricot liqueur
1 papaya, peeled, seeded and diced
1/2 cup apricot nectar
1 cup crushed ice
1 paper umbrella, for garnish
1 maraschino cherry, for garnish

    Combine the rum, liqueur, papaya, apricot nectar, and ice in a blender and blend until smooth. Pour into a tall glass and garnish with a silly umbrella and maraschino cherry.

Yield: 2 servings

Kona Blast

Hawaiian kona coffee is rich, aromatic, and mind-clearing. By itself, it delivers a welcome jolt in the morning. A little rum and coffee liqueur provide an island kick.

1 cup kona coffee
1/8 cup dark rum
1/8 cup coffee liqueur
Whipped cream
1/8 teaspoon ground allspice

Combine the rum, coffee liqueur, and coffee in a cup. Spoon the whipped cream on top and sprinkle with allspice. Serve immediately.

Yield: 1 serving

Java Jive

Jamaica

Jamaican Blue Mountain coffee may be the world's most expensive coffee, but it's worth every penny. Jamaican coffee in the kitchen has always been a strong incentive to rise and shine.

1/4 cup coffee liqueur
1 cup freshly brewed coffee
Whipped cream
1/8 teaspoon ground nutmeg or allspice

Combine the coffee liqueur and coffee in a cup. Spoon the whipped cream on top and sprinkle with nutmeg. Serve immediately.

Yield: 1 serving

INDEX

COOKBOOKS BY THE CROSSING PRESS

Jerk: *Barbecue from Jamaica*
By Helen Willinsky

"An inspired collection of fiery recipes from the Caribbean islands written by an expert on the topic."
—Gourmet Retailer,

"After reading her descriptions I wanted to grab my passport and catch a plane."
—Chile Pepper

$12.95 • Paper • ISBN 0-89594-439-1

Island Cooking: *Recipes from the Caribbean*
By Dunstan Harris

A calypsonian blend of European, African, Indian, Chinese and Native American influences, Caribbean cooking is spicy and satisfying. These recipes represent the cultures and ethnic blends found in the Caribbean.

$10.95 • Paper • ISBN 0-89594-400-6

Traveling Jamaica with Knife, Fork & Spoon
By Robb Walsh and Jay McCarthy

Chef Jay McCarthy and culinary correspondent Robb Walsh take an adventurous trip across the island of Jamaica collecting 140 recipes and meeting dozens of colorful characters along the way.

$16.95 • Paper • ISBN 0-89594-698-X

Fiery Appetizers: *70 Spicy Hot Hors d'Oeuvres*
By Dave DeWitt and Nancy Gerlach

This sizzling collection offers easy-to-follow recipes for seventy spicy-got appetizers guaranteed to satisfy the most discerning of heat-seeking palates.

$8.95 • Paper • ISBN 0-89594-785-4

To receive a current catalog from The Crossing Press
please call toll-free, 800–777–1048.
Visit our Web site: www.crossingpress.com

THE CROSSING PRESS
publishes a full line of cookbooks.
For a free catalog, call toll-free

800 / 777-1048